I0412548

HOW HE WON
WHAT HAPPENS NOW & WHAT TO DO NEXT

BY

TONY PHILLIPS

Kouros Phillips Development, Inc.
425 S. Meadowbrook Drive, 132
San Diego, CA 92114
or
info@kourosphillips.org

Cover photo © Michael Vadon, 2015

For my daughter, whose belief in the possible inspires me.

Acknowledgements

I am grateful to my friends and family for their kind advice and support. Beyond all, I am grateful to my wife and partner, Karen Greene Phillips, for her edits, additions and improvements to this book and for her wisdom in shaping its contents.

"It may well be that we will have to repent in this generation. Not merely for the vitriolic words and the violent actions of the bad people, but for the appalling silence and indifference of the good people who sit around and say, 'Wait on time.'"

Dr. Martin Luther King, Jr.

TABLE OF CONTENTS

Introduction

What many of us thought could not happen did happen. Donald J. Trump, reality television personality, failed casino operator, provocateur, dilletante and tireless self-promoter is the president-elect of the United States. Old school liberals like me are disappointed. Young progressive voters are beyond disappointed. They're angry. Some are frightened. Some feel betrayed by an establishment that paid insufficient attention to their legitimate concerns and they're right to feel as they do.

The result of the 2016 election landed on American progressives like a right uppercut to the jaw, a shot nobody saw coming. As I write this, a week after election night, thousands of protesters are in the streets of major cities on both coasts. The hashtags #notmypresident, #stillwithher and #auditthevote are all among Twitter's most popular. Major print, online and broadcast media outlets have devoted countless hours of coverage to the aftermath of an unforeseen Republican victory and virtually all political pundits, regardless of affiliation, have spent hour after hour addressing one question: "How did this happen?"

There's a short answer to that question, an unsettling one for Democrats and self-identified liberals and progressives. The answer is that President-elect Trump was a better candidate than Hillary Clinton. I hasten to add that "better" is a relative term and in this case, a contextual one. By "better," I don't mean that Trump had superior ideas, or that he had stronger credentials, or more relevant experience, or a deeper understanding of issues, the role of the presidency or, to paraphrase the outgoing President, the world in general. In fact, in each of those areas Trump was, by any objective standard, the inferior candidate. But a candidate's job is to win and by that standard, the only standard that matters, there can be no argument that Donald Trump was *better* than his opponent – very narrowly so, but narrowly better is better enough.

The short answer, he was better, might be sufficient for anyone content with the obvious and resigned to the inevitable. But for politically concerned Americans, the fact that Trump was the better candidate despite his being a worse prospective president raises a

1

second order question: "How did this happen?" This book seeks to answer that question.

My adult daughter, a 27-year-old devout progressive with hard left inclinations, asked me on election night, tearfully, "What do we do now?" I anticipated her call but not the intensity of her emotion. But I was not seeing the election from her perspective. This was her third election. She voted twice before for a decent, classy man of color who won overwhelming victories in a country where his heritage was notable, but not disqualifying. To her, that's what elections were – opportunities to reinforce our common belief in a future better than our past. My daughter grew up in Southern California, spent four university years in Boston and settled in San Jose. She knows that her world is not *the* world but she had never felt the horrible ache in the pit of her stomach that comes with realizing just how much her core values are unimportant to many of her fellow Americans.

As a 50-year-old I'm well used to losing elections. I cast losing votes for Walter Mondale, Michael Dukakis, Al Gore and John Kerry. I'm four-and-five in my voting career. If I were a college football coach I'd be polishing up my resume.

As to my daughter's appeal, what do we do now? I don't have a short answer to that but I do think there are things that can be done. I think the promise of the Millennial generation is very real and very alive and it might be more forcefully awake today than ever before. There is every reason to believe that young progressives will never again be caught napping. I don't believe most young voters took seriously the candidacy of a man who is a veritable caricature of his own worst features. I doubt they will make that mistake in the future.

In this book I ask and attempt to answer what made Trump the better candidate in three key ways. First, to win a presidential election in a country of 350 million people is as much a question of tactics as anything else. What a campaign says, where and to whom it says it, in what words, with what force – all these applied elements of a campaign's message are tactical in nature. Campaign tactics take into account the micro-electorate of regions and sub-regions. They involve consideration of local priorities and values, popular modes of speech and other conventions, and as much as anything else they involve analysis of cost and benefit. Tactics are applied marketing techniques. They are how a candidate sells himself or herself to voters. Trump's tactics beat Clinton's in key states and were a profound lesson to his detractors.

Second, successful campaigns are more often than not characterized by a coherent strategy. Strategy differs from tactics as chess matches differ from moves. Strategy is the overall campaign plan. It involves complex decision-making and activation of organizational plans that lead to tactical execution. As just one example, a campaign's strategy might be to maximize the number of voters who go to the polls. That strategy would entail tactics for getting specific voters to the polls in specific communities, geographic regions, etc. It seemed at times as though Trump had no strategy whatsoever, saying whatever popped into his head and going whichever way the wind blew. That, I suggest, was by design. In fact, Trump's seemingly erratic message *was* his strategy, or at any rate right at the heart of his strategy, one that kept his opponent off-balance and succeeded in directing attention away from the real issues.

Third, there are less tangible elements to be considered in analyzing how Trump won the 2016 election, the sum of which count for as much as his strategy and tactics. They include the intrinsic strengths and weaknesses of each candidate as they relate to widespread voter opinions; various tie-ins, associations and links that connect each candidate to different voter values; and an awareness of the *Zeitgeist*, Georg Hegel's term for the prevailing ideals and beliefs that motivate members of a society at a particular period in time. Trump established himself as the inherently stronger candidate, he connected himself to common voter values and he tapped into the 2016 zeitgeist more decisively than Clinton.

It is important for progressive voters to acknowledge Trump's superiority as a candidate not just to practice humility, but also to learn from this year's myriad mistakes. There could as easily be a Democratic president-elect at this moment. Left-leaning Americans should be encouraged to note that they can win in the future by better executing a sound plan.

Just a week after the election is too soon to paint the full picture of what happened and far too soon to lay blame. I have certainly left out points of view and units of analysis that warrant further consideration and discussion. Facts will continue to roll in and history will tell the final story of the election. My critique in the immediate aftermath of the election is not an attack on the Clinton campaign. I admire the candidate, the campaign, its staff and its vision for the country. I hope my independent analysis adds to the arsenal of progressive candidates to come. Short of that, I hope it answers at least a few nagging questions for those millions of voters who feel betrayed by the outcome of this most recent battle, especially my daughter for whom this book is written.

Trump does not mark the end of the long American liberal tradition and does not represent the death of progress. Progressive liberal values are alive and awakened in the Millennial Generation. There is hope on the horizon and it is embodied by young voters. President Trump might be a current reality, but he need not be an effective or long-lasting one.

How He Won

So it happened. We must all concede the truth – Donald Trump won the election according to the rules. Still, many Americans are bewildered, wondering not just why, but how. Understanding why so many people put their faith in a man with no prior experience or even a clear understanding of government requires piecing together a very big puzzle. But how he won – that's a straightforward question with a clear answer. This section is devoted to addressing that question, perhaps the biggest question of the moment.

In considering how Trump's campaign succeeded we are forced to admit at least two painful truths. First, he just did a better job at running for the presidency than his opponent. That is no doubt the most painful admission of all for anyone who felt invested in the outcome of the vote. Second, at least 60-some million American voters apparently agreed with him and that means young progressives and other anti-Trump citizens are alienated from a large fraction of America. We are forced to conclude that there are at least two Americas – one that believes rancor, hate speech and appeals to our worst tendencies are acceptable in pursuit of high office and one that dos not. We will not likely close that divide in the next four years, if ever. But we can narrow it and the first step toward doing so is examining the election in the most brutally honest terms.

Winning Tactics

Without delving into the dark side of psychology we can rest assured that Trump enjoys conquest. He has told us as much, saying on countless occasions, "I love to win." He has, by his own admission, always put himself and his business ahead of all other concerns. He has bragged about contributing money to both parties and lobbying candidates and public officials for the benefit of his bottom-line. He was a Democrat before he was a Republican.

In pulling off his biggest conquest to date, one that can potentially re-write history and re-frame the accepted world order, Trump used the ample tools at his disposal and he used them to exploit the tactical weakness of his opponent. The Clinton campaign's tactics failed in many ways that Trump successfully exploited. The most important ways are the following.

Clinton's failed message

Team Clinton spoke consistently to a wide audience of Americans and expected the widespread appeal of its message to reach enough voters everywhere to overwhelm Trump's base. Speaking to the widest possible audience is a common Democratic theme. As a candidate, President Obama was fond of saying "We are not a collection of red states and blue states; we are the *United* States..." As a rhetorical device that's a fine sentiment but it's also absolutely untrue. In fact only 12 states out of 50 have vacillated between parties to any degree in the last several elections. Only eight of those are true battleground states. A detailed discussion of the battleground states comes later in this chapter but at this point it is sufficient to note that 38 of 50 states most certainly are not united either by core values or consistent voting patterns.

Twenty-two states have been carried by the Republican candidate in each of the last five presidential elections. There is no reason to believe a broad message to all Americans will register strongly enough with voters in those states to make a difference in the voting booths. Another 16 states have been carried by Democrats in each of the last five elections and the general message of the Clinton campaign obviously spoke strongly to voters in those states.

Unless it's a message that affects voters in the 12, actually eight or, in the case of 2016, six swing states, it's a message that makes no difference. Trump exploited that fact.

Mistaken reliance on facts

The Clinton campaign had an expert candidate, one eminently prepared for the presidency. Clinton's knowledge of policy, her informed insights into actual issues, even her direct experience at multiple levels of government all were assets in blue states and, as it turns out, actual deficits in red states. The campaign routinely cited economic indicators, employment figures and other data as proof that the country was better off following eight years of a Democratic presidency than it was before. The campaign wasted time pointing out that violent crime rates nationally have trended consistently downward for decades. The Brookings Institute reports that "[v]iolent crime has fallen by 51 percent since 1991, and property crime by 43 percent. In 2013 the violent crime rate was the lowest since 1970."[1]

Facts made no difference and for many voters, hammering data points seemed defensive, as if the Clinton campaign was denying their firmly held belief. Many Americans reported feeling less safe, less well off, less you-name-it than at some imagined time in the past and telling them their feelings were wrong, though intended to inform, came off as an insult. In late July 2016, following the Republican Convention, Newt Gingrich summed up the problem with relying on facts in an interview with CNN's Alisyn Camerota saying:

> *"The average American, I will bet you this morning, does not think that crime is down, does not think that we are safer. People feel more threatened. As a political candidate, I'll go with what people feel."*

Trump actually lampooned Clinton for her appeal to facts and used that reliance to underscore the next two of Clinton's tactical failures.

Taking an argumentative tone

To her credit, Clinton could be seen to restrain herself at times in exchanges during three televised debates. She also smiled more during speeches in the last months of the election and tended to use "we" more frequently than "I." All of those accommodations were responsive to criticisms aired in the media, criticisms of Clinton's style. Style matters but so does tone, and by that I don't mean the actual tone of voice Clinton employed, although that is relevant. Clinton's argumentative tone came through in her tendency to challenge Trump's allegations with her own deep well of knowledge. This tendency relates directly to the appeal to facts discussed above, but it is broader than that.

---

[1] "Careful with the Panic: Violent Crime and Gun Crime Are Both Dropping," Charles W. Cooke, *National Review*, November 30, 2015 [retrieved online at nationalreview.com]

At times Clinton insisted on asserting a position in defense of her own knowledge, occasionally repeating herself defiantly, and to voters leaning toward Trump that seemed less like confidence and more like argumentative arrogance. Given that facts don't matter, pushing facts in the face of denial will do nothing but deepen resistance to fact.

In the summer of 2016 I shared this fact on Facebook: *"White non-Hispanics make up 48% of San Diego County's population and 77% of its elected officials. That disparity is actually much better than in many other areas of the country."*

A Facebook friend commented: *"Remove all the illegal immigrants, and the % of population will increase alot [sic]."*

I answered: *"That's factually incorrect. There are 11.4 million undocumented immigrants in the United States...Even if you remove all undocumented Hispanic immigrants White non-Hispanics in the U.S. would increase from 63% to a whopping 64.2%."*

My friend replied: *"1% increase is alot"*

There is no way I was going to convince my friend of anything contrary to his belief that a lot of undocumented immigrants skew American demographics and those reading our exchange probably found me argumentative and high-handed. That's the effect Clinton's insistence on her own correctness had on fence-sitting voters.

Confirming suspicions of elitism

The common thread in the preceding tactical weaknesses was the extent to which the Clinton campaign broadcast a message that many swing state voters read as elitism. It's pedantic of me, I know, but I need to hammer this point. It does not matter that the positions and policies Trump advances will benefit the elite more than the common rung. That is almost certainly true. It is equally true that Clinton's policies would better serve most Americans and do less to advance the interests of the financial elite. Of course that truth *does* matter if we're talking about the consequences of the election. What

I'm saying is that it did not matter to the right voters in the right states, mostly because they didn't believe it.

Common voters in swing states, especially in the Upper Midwest, listened to their own feelings more than facts, tuned out what they thought was pointless argument, and did not respond to a broad, general appeal because they heard all of it as elitist rhetoric.

Opinion polls consistently showed that a majority of voters did not believe Clinton was "honest and trustworthy." It's fair to speculate that a large share of those voters found her dishonest and untrustworthy because they believed she spoke down to them, as if she were dispensing knowledge from on-high, prescribing a course for the country that aligned with her vast experience and privileged perspective. That is the definition of elitism - the belief that an elite class, possessing superior knowledge, can better govern the country than the collective wisdom of the common folk.

While Trump hosted *Saturday Night Live* and let Jimmy Fallon muss his hair on the *Tonight Show*, Clinton was seen as unwilling to make fun of herself. For all Trump's posturing and arrogance, he came across as not taking himself too seriously, a trait that made his exaggerated claims palatable and his espoused arrogance light-hearted. Clinton seemed consistently earnest and professional – two excellent traits in a president, perhaps, but not endearing in a candidate.

Bear in mind we're talking about tactics. I'm not saying that Hillary Clinton is an elitist; I'm saying that a critical mass of voters believed she is.

The above list is not all-inclusive. Yes Hillary Clinton made the mistakes of spreading too broad a message, appealing to facts, and sounding both argumentative and elitist, but there were more gaffes if one wanted to name them. We can say that given all the tactical weaknesses of the Clinton campaign perhaps any Republican candidate could have beaten her. That's open to speculation. What matters for this book is the question of how one particular candidate beat her and following are the principle tactics Trump employed to do so. Two general themes anchored Trump's tactical methods: First, as psychologists delight in telling us, not all human beliefs are rational and second, the media cannot ignore a good story. We should pull these apart before proceeding to the particular elements of Trump's electoral tactics.

Embracing human irrationality
A certain peculiar Austrian wrote in 1935:

> *"The size of the lie is a definite factor in causing it to be believed, for the vast masses of a nation are in the depths of their hearts more easily deceived than they are consciously and intentionally bad. The primitive simplicity of their minds renders them a more easy prey to a big lie than a small one, for they themselves often tell little lies, but would be ashamed to tell big lies."*

Humans are essentially irrational. Scott Adams puts it in less ominous terms on his blog:[2]

> *"If you see voters as rational you'll be a terrible politician. People are not wired to be rational. Our brains simply evolved to keep us alive. Brains did not evolve to give us truth. Brains merely give us movies in our minds that keep us sane and motivated. But none of it is rational or true, except maybe sometimes by coincidence."*

No rational voter could believe that the American electoral system is rigged, especially not in the face of university studies that prove otherwise.[3] No rational voter could believe that this country will build a 30-foot wall along all 1,989 miles of the U.S./Mexico border, much less that Mexico would somehow be made to pay for its construction. No rational voter could believe that this country would either practically or legally enact a "total and complete shutdown of Muslims entering the United States." Statements like those and the countless other outrageous claims Trump made during the campaign are meticulously crafted *not* to appeal to rationality.

---

[2] blog.dilbert.com
[3] "Studies Contradict Trump Claim That Voter Fraud Is 'Very, Very Common'," Associated Press, in *Fortune*, October 18, 2016 [retrieved online at fortune.com]

They are deliberate hyperbole, focused precisely on the least rational aspect of the human mind.

Trump's belligerent statements, all the bellicose slogans and propaganda, the combined force of all his rantings had no basis in fact and that is the very reason they worked. Humans follow feelings more than facts. They reject top-down authority and coercion, they distrust fact-based appeals and elitism and when they go to the polls they follow the irrational part of their mind that responds to demagoguery.

There's no need to get defensive. I don't think that is true of *all* humans. I'm less pessimistic about the human mind than either Scott Adams or the peculiar Austrian. I think it's obvious, however, that at least enough humans are irrational to make a Trump presidency – once unthinkable – a living, terrifying reality.

The media craves a story

It's already hard to remember but there were at one point many Republicans vying for the nomination and Trump seemed like a long-shot to most seasoned observers. In February 2016, 14 different Republicans had spent money on television advertising and, in terms of total spending, Trump ranked sixth out of 14.

Figure 1: Television spending by Republican candidates through February 2016

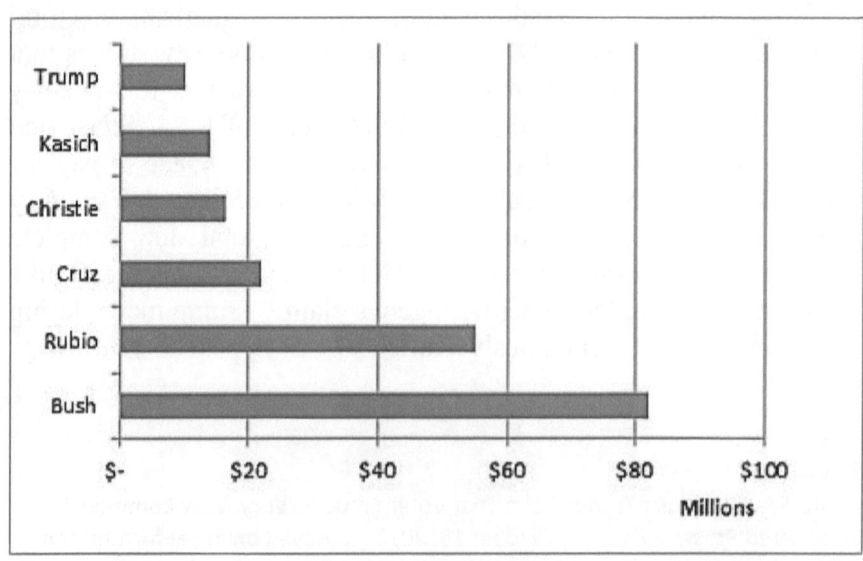

Five Republican candidates, including two U.S. Senators, a sitting governor and two popular former governors outspent Trump in the early stage of the primaries by a combined ratio of nearly 19-to-one. At the time, only three primaries and one caucus had been held and already Trump had won three contests and finished second in the other. At the end of February he led all candidates with 83 delegates compared to 15 for his nearest competitor. Much of Trump's early and ongoing success in the primary and general elections can be attributed to what the industry calls "earned media:" news and commentary about his campaign on television, in newspapers and magazines, and on social media.

In a March 15, 2016, article the *New York Times* reported that through the preceding month Trump had earned almost $2 billion of free media, an amount calculated by the firm MediQuant, which accounts for reach of the media source and includes traditional media of all types, print, broadcast or otherwise, as well as sources like Facebook, Twitter or Reddit. Contrast the chart above with the one below, tracking free media earned by the major Republican candidates.

Figure 2: Earned media coverage for Republican candidates through February 2016

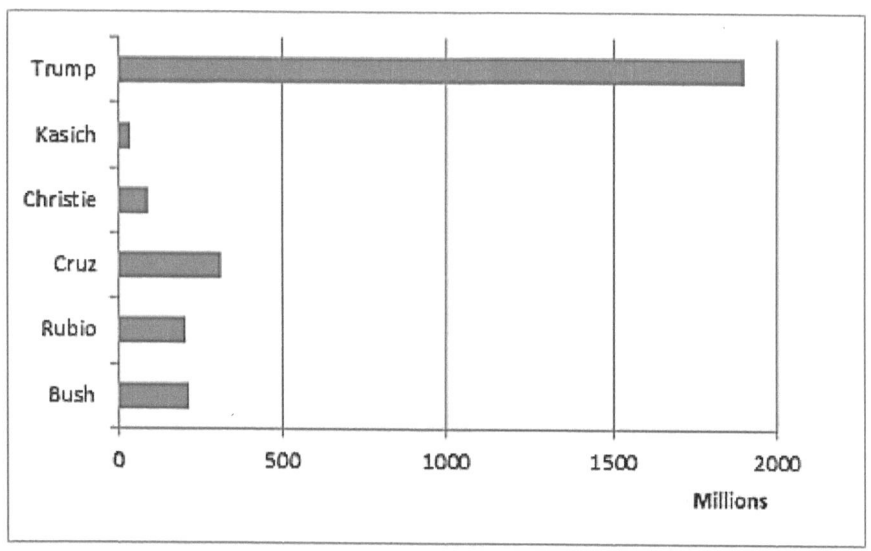

12

Clearly, one major factor in Trump's early dismantling of his Republican opposition was his ability to commandeer the news media. In combined paid and earned media, Trump's presence dwarfed that of Jeb Bush - $2 billion to $296 million. That gap proved insurmountable and as long as Trump remained willing to say anything just to stay in the news, the gap widened. He remained willing, as it turns out, even throughout the general election campaign. By September his earned media for the preceding 12 months exceeded $4.6 billion. By the end of the election it likely topped $10 billion.

It will be observed that much of Trump's coverage was bad, to which I respond with two caveats:

First, "there's no such thing as bad publicity." That sentiment is at least as old as Alexander the Great, the first of a long line of autocrats down to the present day who minted coins bearing their own likeness. The concept must have been known to the Egyptian Pharaohs of the Second Century B.C., who built monuments to their own divinity and inscribed stone walls with apocryphal tales of their great deeds. As far back as one looks in recorded history there are Donald Trumps.

Second, Trump's worst coverage, the coverage that damaged him most in the polls, began with the airing of the *Access Hollywood* video in the first week of October. With barely a month to go before the election, it seemed at the time to be a late-in-the-game surprise Trump would be hard-pressed to overcome. As it turns out it was too late in the game, well past the point at which a critical mass of voters had already taken up the Trump mantle. With those voters' willingness to accept feeling over fact, to reject Clinton as an elitist and a liar, and to buy in to the idea that the whole system was rigged against their candidate, the scandal surrounding Trump's words and actions towards women faded into the background noise of a nasty election battle. What should have been campaign-ending was, in fact, dismissed as part of a clandestine plot to deliver the election to Clinton by acclimation. Such is the irrationality of the human mind.

Thus altogether the American media, conventional and otherwise, was Donald Trump's chief weapon in out-messaging his opponents and he used that weapon ruthlessly and exhaustively. Marshall McLuhan wrote that the medium is the message. Neil

Postman was more long-winded on the topic, writing in the introduction to his seminal book, *Amusing Ourselves to Death*:

> *"What Orwell feared were those who would ban books. What Huxley feared was that there would be no reason to ban a book, for there would be no one who wanted to read one. Orwell feared those who would deprive us of information. Huxley feared those who would give us so much that we would be reduced to passivity and egoism. Orwell feared that the truth would be concealed from us. Huxley feared the truth would be drowned in a sea of irrelevance. Orwell feared we would become a captive culture. Huxley feared we would become a trivial culture, preoccupied with some equivalent of the feelies, the orgy porgy, and the centrifugal bumblepuppy. As Huxley remarked in* Brave New World Revisited, *the civil libertarians and rationalists who are ever on the alert to oppose tyranny 'failed to take into account man's almost infinite appetite for distractions.'"*

In amplifying his overall message, Postman wrote later that "Americans no longer talk to each other, they entertain each other. They do not exchange ideas, they exchange images. They do not argue with propositions; they argue with good looks, celebrities and commercials."

Indeed, the media cannot resist a story. Covering stories, especially stories like Donald Trump, is woven into the fiber of what the media are. The media are an interconnected hive-mind that perpetuates memes and clips and soundbites and can't stop itself from doing so. Even if, for the sake of argument, various news outlets wanted to dismantle Trump by dissecting his dishonesty, his evocation of racism, sexism, Islamophobia, xenophobia, homophobia and other bigotry, even if those outlets wished to document his complete lack of qualification or experience, even if they wanted to note his manifest character and temperament flaws, in order to do so they had to talk about him and that's the rub. The opposite of love is not hate, it is indifference, and the opposite of praise is not criticism, but silence. The media can be neither indifferent to nor silent about a story like Donald Trump and that fact makes the media an assault rifle in Trump's hands.

It is quite probable that no human being has ever received more publicity in a single year than Donald Trump – not Elvis, not O.J., not J.F.K.

***

Following the two preceding themes – reliance on human irrationality and the media's insatiable appetite for a story, Trump employed several tactics to achieve three general strategic goals: 1) driving his own voters to the polls, 2) suppressing voter turnout for his opponent and 3) converting disenchanted Democrats and independents to his side. We will revisit these goals in the following chapter but first let us look at Trump's major tactics.

Beating the drum
A byproduct of human irrationality is the willingness to fall in line behind a leader whose message is loud and rhythmic. Trump beat the drum for a year-and-a-half, echoing his own message over and over, relentlessly, loudly, following a scripted meter that had no real melody, just a thunderous beat. This was most evident at his rallies, each one indistinguishable from all others. The transcripts of his rally speeches are practically nonsensical and even when they are more or less coherent they dwell on a central theme – There is a vast array of corrupt power centers joined in an unholy alliance to deprive you, the American people from prosperity and I alone can fix it. He makes it life and death, sounding alarm bells about cultural genocide, attacks on Christianity, Washington seizing citizens' guns (their last line of defense against Washington crusaders), and stacking the Supreme Court with scofflaws. Consider the following examples.

> *"Our movement is about replacing a failed and corrupt — now, when I say 'corrupt,' I'm talking about totally corrupt — political establishment, with a new government controlled by you, the American people. There is nothing the political establishment will not do — no lie that they won't tell, to hold their*

15

prestige and power at your expense. And that's what's been happening."

And

    "The establishment has trillions of dollars at stake in this election. As an example, just one single trade deal they'd like to pass involves trillions of dollars, controlled by many countries, corporations and lobbyists. For those who control the levers of power in Washington, and for the global special interests, they partner with these people that don't have your good in mind. Our campaign represents a true existential threat like they haven't seen before."

And

    "The political establishment that is trying to stop us is the same group responsible for our disastrous trade deals, massive illegal immigration and economic and foreign policies that have bled our country dry. The political establishment has brought about the destruction of our factories, and our jobs, as they flee to Mexico, China and other countries all around the world. Our just-announced job numbers are anemic. Our gross domestic product, or GDP, is barely above 1 percent. And going down. Workers in the United States are making less than they were almost 20 years ago, and yet they are working harder."

And finally,

    "But so am I working harder, that I can tell you."

The foregoing is pure Trumpism, delivered in the opening two minutes of a single speech at a rally in Florida 26 days before the election, a week after the *Access Hollywood* story dominated the airwaves. Note the repetition – using the word "establishment" twice and "corrupt" thrice in a single sentence. Repetition has the effect of imprinting on the human mind, hence "corrupt political establishment" becomes a meme with a life of its own.

Similarly the repetition of "trillions," used twice in a span of words to emphasize the wealth supposedly at stake in the corrupt establishment's evil game to oppress real Americans. For reference, the total annual budget of the United States is $3.6 trillion. There is no cabal of malevolent special interests that control as much wealth as the federal government and to imagine such a group strains credulity. But in 2016 "billions of dollars" lacks the force of exaggeration and mass outrage is more easily stoked by "trillions." Again, facts don't matter.

He invokes two foreign countries long demonized in his own rhetoric. Mexico is sending us rapists and China is raping our country. Note the mis-statement, that our GDP is barely above one percent. In fact he meant the *growth* of our GDP, presumably, and at any rate the figure is inaccurate. The U.S. GDP grew by 2.5% in 2015, slightly outpacing the rest of the world combined, Mexico and China included.

He mentions U.S. workers and commiserates with them about working harder and earning less. Median household incomes in the country increased by $2,800 from 2014 to 2015 and adjusted for inflation median incomes are $3,100 higher than in 1996. Americans work an average of 34.4 hours per week. Twenty years ago they worked 34.6 hours. In 1966 they worked 38 hours. So there is not a single fact buried anywhere in his firm declaration, but he declared it nonetheless and added himself to the equation – "So am I working harder," marking the "us/them" distinction and lining up on the "us" side. The irony of such a claim from a billionaire who did nothing but promote himself on television for 18 months was lost entirely on the Florida crowd.

It's easy to disparage Trump for the vacuity of his speech-making or the complete falseness of his premises. But to disparage him altogether is to miss a critical point: it worked.

Appealing to emotion
Having dispensed entirely with facts and embraced human irrationality, Trump was free to speak purely to human emotion, that most powerful of forces. Adams writes in his blog:

17

"The evidence is that Trump completely ignores reality and rational thinking in favor of emotional appeal. Sure, much of what Trump says makes sense to his supporters, but I assure you that is coincidence. Trump says whatever gets him the result he wants. He understands humans as 90-percent irrational and acts accordingly. People vote based on emotion. Period."

Trump's convention address in July was a veritable prophecy of impending doom. In addressing critics who observed that the speech was "dystopic" and "negative," *Salon*'s Chauncey DeVega wrote:

"Of course, it was. This is by design. Donald Trump understands the political personalities and brain structures of his conservative-authoritarian supporters. The latter are fear-centered in their thinking, fixate on disturbing and ugly images, and are easily manipulated by death anxieties."

DeVega adds:

"Trump is a strongman and proto fascist. He describes a 'problem' in society and offers himself as the only solution. Trump's conservative-authoritarian supporters seek out strong father figures and other saviors. They are also prone to social dominance behavior and hostility to people who are different from them. Donald Trump is their avatar, a bully who will protect them from (imagined) threats and a 'scary' world."

Not all human emotions are created equal. Our primary emotions include fear, anger, sadness and happiness and these emotions motivate our actions in more or less that order, with fear being the most potent of all emotions at evoking a response. There is a survival advantage in our sensitivity to fear but played upon by a

Svengali like Trump, fear is a betrayer – handing us over to the wiles of the will-shaper.

At one point in the campaign, Trump was called out for an inaccurate tweet by none other than Fox News's Bill O'Reilly. O'Reilly cited a graphic shared by Trump in November 2015 attributed to the non-existent "Crime Statistics Bureau – San Francisco. The graphic purported that 81% of homicides involved Whites killed by Blacks. Even O'Reilly couldn't let such a claim go unchallenged, noting that the official FBI statistics for the prior full year put the figure at 15% 5.4 times lower than Trump's tweet.

November 2015 was a trying time in White-Black relations. Black unemployment at the time of Trump's tweet was 10.9%, twice the national rate at the time. Blacks made up 37% of the male prison population and only 6% of the male population overall. Black males between the ages of 15 and 34 made up only 2% of the total population but accounted for 15% of all deaths at the hands of law enforcement officers. Public unrest and at times violent protests broke out in many cities in the wake of multiple shootings of unarmed Black suspects.

All in all it was a perfect time for a man unconstrained by decency to propagate a myth about Black-on-White violence, a phenomenon that is quite uncommon. And despite its proven inaccuracy the tweet had the desired effect. It furthered a lingering fear that roils near the surface of American public life – fear of the "Black Savage."

Trump disclaimed his responsibility for the tweet telling O'Reilly, "All I know is what's on the internet," an excuse so feeble one might laugh at it, except that it is really no excuse at all. One can surmise Trump didn't really care about the accuracy of the claim, as long as it pumped up the fear already activated, especially in the nation's heartland where Blacks make up a disproportionately low share of the population. It is easier to fear that which one does not know.

The use of fear as a means of public manipulation has a long, ugly history. Most recently Americans saw the George W. Bush administration create a color-coded terror alert scale. Much has been written about that administration's fear-based public messaging. What the Bush team achieved was the statutory suspension of fundamental civil liberties through the Patriot Act, the bi-partisan endorsement of a war against a country that had never attacked or threatened to attack us, a clandestine government program of domestic surveillance and the collection of an unprecedented store of communication records from virtually all Americans, and a Justice Department that formally endorsed and condoned the use of torture in contravention of multiple international treaties.

Donald Trump is even more brazen in his use of fear to bait an unwitting public than was President Bush.

One of the single most important results of Trump's use of emotion, combined with his belligerent statements about women, minorities and other historically disempowered groups, was his emergence as a perceived Alpha Male by 73% of White male voters. This perception crossed over to White female voters who, defying all expectations, cast 53% of their votes for Trump compared to 43% for Clinton. That bears repeating – White women cast 10% more votes for a man who said his stardom entitled him to "grab women by the pussy" than for a vastly more qualified woman candidate.

It's important at this point to note that Trump's adoption of the Alpha Male mantle appealed to voters emotions. Their emotional acceptance of his posturing allowed them to thoroughly reject qualifications, experience and all other relevant considerations based in real facts.

Being error-proof
Trump, quite famously, does not apologize or correct himself. He says what he says and does what he does. If it is proven wrong or criticized as insensitive, he shrugs and moves on. Refusing to concede his own fallibility is one of Trump's defining traits and it stands in clear distinction to all presidents in living memory.

Adams writes:

> *"If you are not trained in persuasion, Trump looks stupid, evil, and maybe crazy. If you understand persuasion, Trump is pitch-perfect most of the time. He ignores unnecessary rational thought and objective data and incessantly hammers on what matters (emotions).*
>
> *Did Trump's involvement in the birther thing confuse you? Were you wondering how Trump could*

believe Obama was not a citizen? The answer is that
Trump never believed anything about Obama's place
of birth. The facts were irrelevant, so he ignored them
while finding a place in the hearts of conservatives.
For later.
This is later. He plans ahead."

Following the tragic mass shooting at the Bataclan in Paris in November 2015, Trump called for shutting down mosques in this country, telling Fox News:

"Nobody wants to say this and nobody wants to
shut down religious institutions or anything, but you
know, you understand it. A lot of people understand
it. We're going to have no choice,"

Trump never rescinded that sentiment. Neither the president nor any public official in the U.S. has the authority to close down any religious institution, but in Trump's universe his statement was an obvious truism. He said it and that in and of itself made it so – a speech act capable of occasioning into existence a kernel of thought that could be construed however one wanted. That it was construed hatefully, with malice and distrust, by a great number of Americans who harbor anti-Islamic sentiments was not Trump's fault insofar as he was "just saying what a lot of people think."

A man who styles himself as the only solution to a sea of ills cannot be subject to error. What he says, even if he contradicts it later, is never wrong. To apologize for his mistakes would be to break character and the character of an infallible, all-powerful Trump is at the core of his entire persona, a cornerstone of his public life and political aspiration.

Identity politics

Let us deal with an important fact – identity involves much more than race. It would be easy to follow pundits and commentators who attribute Trump's ascendancy to White voters' prejudice and antipathy to minority groups but that would be overly simplistic. To focus exclusively on racial prejudice, which definitely exists, is to ignore the flip-side of White identity, which is a conscious attempt to preserve and defend White interests in an increasingly pluralistic America. Racial prejudice as we commonly think of it consists of negative attitudes toward other groups. But the White identity tapped into by Trump had more to do with a collective sense of connection between White Americans. In a nutshell, the White identity politics that served Trump most was not anti-minority, it was pro-majority.

The difference is thin. I'm aware that drawing the distinction might be interpreted as missing something, namely that pro-White almost by definition is anti-everyone else. Unchecked promotion of the majority identity does, intentionally or otherwise, fail to recognize the points of view present in the plural minority. I recognize that fact and I believe that only from a position of privilege could a majority ignore that promoting its own culture necessarily means overlooking others. However, while that no doubt is the case, it does not follow that most White voters *believed* it to be the case.

Trump, whose earliest major campaign plank was "Build the wall," won 29% of the Hispanic vote and 8% of the Black vote. Both those figures were higher than for Mitt Romney in 2012. It is no doubt true that overt White racists voted for Trump, but their numbers weren't sufficient to win the election. In fact, millions of White voters who voted for Trump voted twice for a Black man whose middle name is Hussein.

For now, the type of identity politics that relates to Trump's tactics is the creation of an Alpha Male image and the magnetism of that image for Republican and independent voters, male and female alike. In the spring of 2016, Adams wrote:

> *"Identity is always the strongest level of persuasion. The only way to beat it is with dirty tricks or a stronger identity play. Trump is well on his way to owning the identities of Alpha Males, and Women Who Like Alpha Males. Clinton is well on her way to owning the identities of angry women, beta males, immigrants, and disenfranchised minorities.*
>
> *If this were poker, which hand looks stronger to you for a national election?"*

In May 2016, CNN contributor Van Jones, a former aide to President Obama, current President of Dream Corps, and 2010 recipient of the NAACP's President's Award, warned viewers and fellow CNN personalities that Trump "probably will win the presidency." Jones did not get lucky with his dire prognostication; he saw what was happening.

Jones insisted that Trump was not merely defying the old rules of political campaigns; he was instead defining the new rules of a game he could win. He listed Trump's use of social media, his command of the reality television phenomenon and his ability to cast himself in a light that appealed even to Black voters.

In a Facebook post, Jones wrote, "Everything that Trump is doing conforms to the rules of social media. You don't get fewer followers when you insult somebody... or say something outrageous on Twitter, you get more followers."

Jones was especially intent on pointing to Trump's support among Black voters, saying, "Seventy percent of African-Americans have a horrible view of Donald Trump. In order for the Democrats to win the White House they don't have to get 50 percent of the Black vote or 60, or 70, or 80, or 90. Democrats, in order to win historically, need 90 to 92 percent of the Black vote." As he saw it, if only 70% of Black voters strongly opposed Trump, 30% must be open to his argument and "if he gets half of those, he's president." At the time of his remarks, Public Policy Polling data showed that 15% of Black voters in swing state Ohio supported Trump over Clinton, with another 11% undecided. That contrasts with Romney's 4% of Ohio's Black vote in 2012. Trump eventually won 8% of the Black vote nationwide.

Trump appealed to the masses as a man not afraid to say what is on his mind and for many voters, even some Black voters, that quality was a deciding factor in a contest between two candidates about each of whom they had serious doubts. Trump's willingness to make his campaign all about him, his rejection of polite speech and the normal conventions of public discourse, his bullying tweets and soundbites, his name-calling and ad hominem attacks all made him seem both stronger and more authentic. Coming off as unpolished and unpracticed was a boon to his image, giving him the advantage of sounding spontaneous and genuine by comparison to Clinton's rehearsed style.

Spontaneity and unguarded self-assurance are two features of the archetypal Alpha Male that attracted voters who sought to identify with Trump's image. It is in that regard that identity politics played its primary role in Trump's campaign tactics – drawing in voters who identified with his flagrant disregard for basic courtesy, welcoming each crass remark and put-down of an establishment from which voters already felt estranged. Most Americans at times wish they could insult a political leader, a media figure or an entire institution. Trump did it for them.

Trump's identity became voters' identities, a fact on display at his rallies where supporters felt emboldened to act out, sometimes violently, to suppress detractors' protests or mere presence. Adams notes that Trump's favored linguistic kill shots had two qualities: they involve a fresh word not generally used in politics and they aim at the physicality of the subject.

Trump coined "Little Marco," "Low-energy Jeb," and "Goofy Elizabeth Warren," the latter of which he later ditched in favor of "Pocahontas." In his most notorious invocation of physicality as an insult he mocked the *Washington Post*'s Serge Kovaleski, who suffers from arthrogryposis, which limits the movement of his joints and is especially noticeable in his right arm and hand. Trump has never apologized for (or even admitted to) mimicking and ridiculing Kovaleski, a distinguished journalist and co-recipient of a Pulitzer Prize, among other distinctions earned in a 30-year career.

To be sure there are plenty of other Alpha Males who are unmoved by Trump's puffed-chest posturing. President Obama, Vice President Biden and Senate Minority Leader Harry Reid leap to mind, along with Mitt Romney, John McCain and both Presidents Bush. But in Trump's redefined universe, even leaders of strong character who have challenged and stood against him have eventually been brought to heel. House Speaker Paul Ryan, who just wasn't there yet about endorsing Trump before the GOP Convention, who told fellow Congressional Republicans they should feel free to reject Trump and who refused to campaign with Trump right up to Election Day, appeared with the entire Republican Caucus a week after the election wearing a "Make America Great Again" hat and welcoming reporters to a press conference by saying, "Welcome everybody to the dawn of a new, unified, Republican government."

In an even more dramatic flip-flop than Ryan's, Texas Senator Ted Cruz, who refused to endorse Trump from the floor of the Convention and who told reporters, "I am not in the habit of endorsing someone who attacks my wife and attacks my father," eventually did endorse Trump and campaign on his behalf. Within a week of the election, Cruz visited Trump Tower for an audience with the President-elect, a man who, months earlier, tweeted an unflattering photo of Cruz's wife alongside a photo of Mrs. Trump, a European fashion model who is 24 years Trump's junior.

At the moment, Mitt Romney remains in contention for appointment as Secretary of State and has met twice with Trump, even dining with him at a swank Manhattan restaurant.

We can say he's not a real Alpha Male, but Trump has managed to pull plenty of other strong men in line behind him. Adams cut to the heart of the apparent conundrum that is Trump's domination by insult:

> *"Do you think it is a coincidence that Trump called Megyn Kelly a bimbo and then she got a non-bimbo haircut that is ... well, Trumpian. It doesn't look like a coincidence to [a] trained persuader."*

One week after the election, heads of state from several long-time U.S. allies reported through back channels that they had been unable to reach Trump by phone, one resorting to calling the switchboard at Trump Tower. Sources within the U.S. State Department confirmed that Trump's team had not worked with the Department to follow long-established protocol in connecting with foreign leaders. However, Trump himself boasted that he had been in touch with other nations' chief executives, tweeting on November 16, 2016, "I have received and taken calls from many foreign leaders despite what the failing @nytimes said. Russia, U.K., China, Saudi Arabia, Japan."

Trump also received public acclimation and encouragement from a few leaders, among them Vladimir Putin, Bashar Assad and Rodrigo Duterte. Putin's despotism needs no embellishment. Assad, at the time of this writing, is waging a sixth year of civil war in which he has used poison gas against his own citizens. On November 15, Assad's ally, Putin, ordered Russian forces to resume their bombing of the besieged Syrian city of Aleppo in advance of an announced major joint offensive.

The Philippines' Duterte was elected after supporting the extrajudicial killing of drug users while serving as the mayor of Davao City. Duterte has bragged to reporters about shooting a fellow law student in the 1970s over alleged racial insults. At a campaign rally in April 2016, he recalled examining the corpse of an Australian missionary who was gang-raped and killed in the 1989 Davao hostage crisis, telling the audience of thousands:

> *"When the bodies were brought out, they were wrapped. I looked at her face, son of a bitch, she looks like a beautiful American actress. Son of a bitch, what a waste. What came to mind was, they raped her, they lined up. I was angry because she was raped? Yes, that's one thing. But she was so beautiful! I think the mayor should have been first. What a waste."*

All three men and other strongmen around the world are lined up to welcome Trump to their fraternity. Assad called Trump a "natural ally" in the fight against terrorism. Trump's identity politics have effectively crossed the world's oceans and would-be Caesars are eager to identify themselves with him. Humans are irrational and identity politics work.

Complete domination
The combination of Trump's tactics – his exploitation of human irrationality, his mastery of the media including new media forms, his constant beating of the drum, his appeal to emotion, his refusal to admit error and his use of identity politics – overwhelmed Clinton's more conventional tactics with an outcome that was fatal to Clinton's voter appeal. I will note that Clinton received more votes, 62.3 million, than Trump, 61.2 million, beating him by a margin of 47.8% to 46.9%.[4] Her popular vote victory is historic – never before

---

[4] Vote totals used throughout this book are current as of November 16, 2016. They may change by a fraction of a percent as individual states arrive at their final, certified tallies.

has a candidate won the popular vote by so wide a margin and lost the electoral vote. Nevertheless the 2016 election was the second election of five in the current century in which a Democratic candidate won the popular vote and lost the election.

The 2016 results are shown graphically in the map on the following page:

There are more than 3,100 individual data points corresponding to individual counties and county equivalents (parishes, boroughs, census areas and independent cities) represented in the contiguous states. The darker the county, the more Clinton votes were cast there.[5] The most obvious feature of the map is its lack of uniformity. There are mostly grey regions with a large swath of nearly white. There are also speckles of almost black, most of which correspond to major urban areas, college towns and state capitals. No matter how you look at it, the map looks nothing like an overwhelming Trump victory (see following page).

---

[5] The nearly black area in lower South Dakota is Oglala Lakota County, located entirely within the Pine Ridge Indian Reservation. Oglala Lakota has the highest rate of premature death of any county in the country. The median annual household income in Oglala Lakota is less than $21,000, compared to the national average of almost $56,000. Oglala Lakota County does not have its own county seat. Its administrative center is located in Hot Springs in neighboring Fall River County. The people of Oglala Lakota County voted for Clinton over Trump 86.5% to 8.3%. Their total of 2,896 votes were drowned out, however, in the rest of the state, where Trump won with 61.5% to Clinton's 31.7%. Democracy alone will not protect a vulnerable minority from the tyranny of the majority.

Figure 3: Distribution of Clinton votes by percentage in individual counties

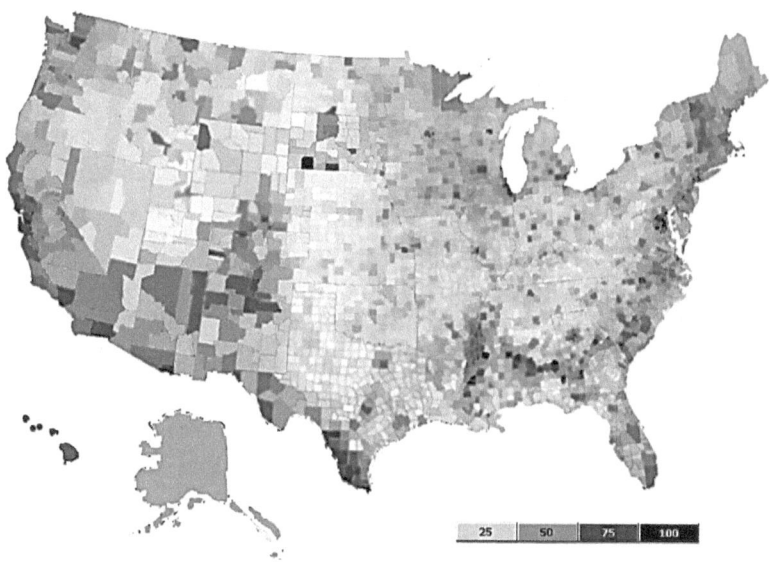

But in the perverse arithmetic of American presidential elections, the most popular candidate does not necessarily win. Trump's margin of electoral victory, 290-232, is wider even than George W. Bush's margin over Al Gore in 2000, 271-266, when Gore won just over 500,000 more popular votes than Bush. Trump's victory over an opponent who defeated him by more than 2 million votes is without any historical precedent. He did not just squeak out a win over Clinton; he demolished her, despite her convincing win at nationwide polls.

Clinton carried historically blue states overwhelmingly. In California she beat Trump 61.5% to 33.2%. In Massachusetts the margin was 60.8% to 33.5% and in Vermont it was 61.1% to 32.6%. In Washington D.C. Clinton's victory margin was an astounding 92.8% to 4.1%. Trump's margin in reliably red states was convincing, but in the most populous of those states his margin was considerably narrower than Clinton's in her blue strongholds. But margins don't matter. In all states except Maine and Nebraska, electoral votes are allocated on an all-or-nothing basis. As a result, a 99-1 victory is worth no more than a 51-49 victory.

That is what makes swing states the highest stakes in the presidential game, honestly the only states that matter. The political website FiveThirtyEight identifies the states of Colorado, Florida, Iowa, Michigan, Minnesota, Nevada, New Hampshire, North Carolina, Ohio, Pennsylvania, Virginia and Wisconsin as "perennial " swing states where elections have been consistently close for the past several cycles. Trump won seven of those states and Clinton won five, dividing their combined electoral votes 114 to 42, respectively.

A win in Florida and any other state on the list would have delivered the election to Clinton, as would wins in two of any out of three among Michigan, Ohio and Pennsylvania. Clinton lost six states that Obama won in 2012. These were the states that turned the election: Florida, Iowa, Michigan, Ohio, Pennsylvania and Wisconsin. The margin of victory for Trump in four of those states – Florida, Michigan, Pennsylvania and Wisconsin was 1.3% or less. Only Iowa and Ohio were major Trump swing state victories. Altogether, between six blue states turned red, Trump won 14,778,051 to Clinton's 13,948,249, a difference of less than 830,000.

To flip the outcome of the election, the shortest route would be for Clinton to have kept Michigan and Pennsylvania in the blue column. Trump took those contests by a combined 79,659 votes. So when all is said and done, there were some 130 million votes cast for President in the 2016 election and the outcome turned on fewer than 80,000 in two states that comprise less than 7% of the country's population.

Some Presidents are elected by a majority; others are anointed by a few.

This is not new. Four times in our history the winner of the popular vote has lost in the Electoral College.[6] The most lopsided popular vote in any presidential election was Lyndon Johnson's 61.1% share in 1964. Since that time five of 13 elections have been won by a candidate who received less than 50% of the popular vote. Bill Clinton achieved that feat twice, winning in 1992 with 43.01%

---

[6] My friend and associate, Fred Rogers, a seasoned political consult, campaign advisor and San Diego Democratic Party Central Committee member, refers to the Electoral College as "the last vestige of American Slavocracy."

of the vote and in 1996 with 49.23%. In both cases, however, he trounced his opponents, winning the Electoral College vote 370-168 and 379-159.

Summary of tactics

This year a man who lied, insulted and bullied his opposition, threatened reprisals against his detractors including members of the news media, derided the entire American electoral process as a rigged system, engaged in thinly veiled racism, pledged to exclude an entire faith of more than a billion people from the country, was accused by more than a dozen women of sexual assault and consistently refused to apologize or take responsibility for his own actions or those of his followers rose to the most powerful position in the world by swinging a few counties in a few states. Some truly insightful people saw it coming. Many of us did not.

One of two things is true: either Donald Trump is a genius or he got blind lucky. Actually I think there is some truth to both those possibilities. There is something else that I think: almost by definition a man who will lie about anything, refuse to apologize, deny his own past words and actions, bully and insult weaker people and laugh about it all either is a psychopath or is good at acting like one. It doesn't really matter which is the case; psychopathy is as psychopathy does. In this instance the generous thing is to assume that Trump is a normal person who merely used psychopathic means to achieve a Machiavellian end.

The country and the world came infuriatingly close to a different outcome, despite Trump's mastery of tactics. If the above numbers aren't persuasive about that point we can (and will) consult maps of swing states that note down to the individual counties where the entire election was won and lost. As difficult as this all may be to accept, it comes with the slightly optimistic news that it didn't have to happen. Just a slight change in any one of a dozen or more variables would have changed it all. The even better news is that knowing those variables, there is no reason it should happen again.

<u>Winning Strategy</u>
There can be no doubt that Trump as a candidate excelled at tactics that achieved three outcomes: 1) dividing opinion, 2) converting swing voters and 3) keeping key demographics at home. On election night, sources inside Trump's own camp told CNN "it would take a miracle for us to win." There is some doubt whether even Trump himself believed his proclamations of impending victory. He seemed to be positioning himself to blame a rigged system for Clinton's almost certain win.

On November 10, the American Association for Public Opinion Research said in an emailed statement:

> *"Election years present particularly high profile moments for public opinion and survey research. This is a time when polls dominate the media and the accuracy of polls can be confirmed or refuted by the actual poll vote outcome. The polls clearly got it wrong this time and Donald J. Trump is the projected winner in the Electoral College... There is much speculation today about what led to these errors and already the chorus of concerns about a 'crisis in polling' have emerged as headlines on news and social media sites... [U]nderstanding and being able to articulate the overall outcomes of election polling, the changing methodologies being used, and the potential for variation in the accuracy of polls is vital for the industry."*

A case could be made for the polls sharing some blame for Clinton's loss. All major polls had her ahead going into Election Day by at least three points and most had her leading by four points or more. Perhaps, with an assurance of victory dominating the airwaves, less than enthusiastic Clinton voters thought it was in the bag and skipped the voting booths. It is evident that turnout was lower than expected among a few key demographics.

For those not content to blame an abstraction, FBI Director James Comey is a popular human target. Comey's vague memo to Congress about the possible continuation of an investigation into Clinton's use of a private email server came to light on October 28,

11 days before the election. Democrats had no time left to kill a non-story about an issue that had been fully aired for more than a year. However, satisfying though it may feel to blame the nation's top cop for vote tampering, Comey did not cost Clinton the election.

At a post-election meeting at Democratic Party headquarters a young staffer identified only as Zach lambasted interim DNC Chair Donna Brazile shouting, "Why should we trust you as chair to lead us through this? You backed a flawed candidate, and your friend [former DNC chair Debbie Wasserman Schultz] plotted through this to support your own gain and yourself." Zach went on, "You are part of the problem," blaming Brazile for siding with Clinton early in the primary season. "You and your friends will die of old age and I'm going to die from climate change. You and your friends let this happen, which is going to cut 40 years off my life expectancy."

Zach might have a valid point. The internal shenanigans and foul play of the DNC uncovered in a seemingly unending drip of Wiki-leaked emails lent some credence to Trump's suggestion that Clinton was part of a rigged system. Still, that in and of itself can't account for Clinton's loss. Not even all the above put together really capture the full picture.

On November 16 *The Huffington Post*'s Sam Stein wrote:

> "*Several theories have been proffered to explain just what went wrong for the Clinton campaign in an election that virtually everyone expected the Democratic nominee to win. But lost in the discussion is a simple explanation, one that was re-emphasized to* HuffPost *in interviews with several high-ranking officials and state-based organizers: The Clinton campaign was harmed by its own neglect.*
>
> *In Michigan alone, a senior battleground state operative told* HuffPost *that the state party and local officials were running at roughly one-tenth the paid canvasser capacity that Sen. John Kerry (D-Mass.) had when he ran for president in 2004. Desperate for more human capital, the state party and local officials ended up raising $300,000 themselves to pay 500 people to help canvass in the election's closing weeks. By that point, however, they were operating in*

the dark. One organizer said that in a precinct in Flint, they were sent to a burned down trailer park. No one had taken it off the list of places to visit because no one had been there until the final weekend. Clinton lost the state by 12,000 votes."

Furthermore, wrote Stein:

"The more universal explanation... was that the data that informed many of the strategic decisions was simply wrong. A campaign that is given a game plan that strongly points to success shouldn't be expected to rip it up.
'We all were blinded, and even at the end, we were blinded by our own set of biases,' said Paul Maslin, a Madison-based Democratic operative and pollster."

It may yet turn out that Clinton was not only perceived as arrogant, but that her campaign truly was arrogant and smugly content to rest on its rock-solid "blue wall," a wall that Trump shattered. What did not shatter was the imitation glass ceiling Clinton had installed over her U.S. map-shaped stage at the hall rented for her victory speech. That got packed up and shipped off in silence while sincere believers were left with no words at all from Clinton until the following day at a small gathering. In a touch of humility that came a day too late, Clinton was the first losing candidate on record to say the words, "I'm sorry," to supporters in a concession speech.

Clinton's campaign strategy was straightforward. Central to that strategy were undercutting Trump's character and temperament, emphasizing her own qualifications and experience, running on Obama's record and popularity, promoting herself as a new-fangled progressive, and not so subtly pointing out the historic opportunity to elect a woman president. Those major themes were intended to maximize voter turnout among historically under-represented minority groups, capture the lion's share of the female vote, draw young voters – Obama and Sanders voters – to the polls, and hold onto White working-class voters in the Rust Belt. She accomplished none of those major strategic goals.

During the primary campaigns practically any on-air pundit (other than Van Jones) who offered an opinion speculated that Trump would be the one Republican Clinton would most want to run against. That speculation centered on Trump's abysmal unfavorable opinion numbers in nationwide polls and the reasoning that Clinton, with her depth and breadth of policy and issue knowledge, would trounce an opponent who was comparatively ignorant about Washington matters.

By the end of July, however, the two candidates' poll numbers were roughly even and Clinton advocates had begun to concede they had a fight on their hands. Geoff Garin, a pollster and strategist with Clinton's unsuccessful 2008 campaign told the *Wall Street Journal* on July 28, "I fully expect this to be a close and competitive election all the way to the end."

Former RNC chairman Michael Steele joined Jones in disagreeing with received opinion saying, "This is not an election about policy and ideology. It's an election about, 'What do I think of you as a leader.' She has a lot of qualifications, but they just don't trust her or like her. That's hard to overcome."

Hindsight, like the next presidential election, is 20/20.

Clinton's strategy failed her in the end. That fact is certain, but to say Clinton failed is to ignore an equally important converse fact, which is that Trump won. In fact, the inevitable dissection that will consume Democratic strategists in months to come would overlook at the party's peril the reality that their candidate did not lose to a phantom. There was another fighter in the ring and it is my contention and firm belief that the election turned more on the success of his strategy than on the failure of hers.

There is nothing intrinsically wrong with Clinton's central strategic themes. No matter what else she might have added to them the truth is she was engaged in a steeper uphill climb than most progressives could see. There have been 58 presidential elections and only six times has a candidate won from the same party as a two-term incumbent. It has not happened since 1988. Prior to that one has to go back to Harry Truman in 1948. Voters like change.

It is also true without a doubt that a certain amount of anti-woman bias, conscious or unconscious, lingers in the minds of many

American voters. As a society we have become so inclusive in our outward speech and actions it's easy to ignore the deep sentiments that abide in our private thoughts. While a majority of Americans surveyed in a plethora of polls will say they believe there is no difference in the leadership qualities of women and men, women make up only slightly more than 15% of chief executives at *Fortune* 500 companies. Women are roughly 53% of the total U.S. electorate and yet the 114th Congress has 20 women Senators out of 100 and 106 women Representatives out of 453.

Again, however, institutional issues alone did not sink the Clinton campaign, any more than an imperfect strategy did. Trump's campaign was simply better.

Use of polls

The Trump campaign early on was willing to disregard and flatly reject the accuracy of opinion polls. That he was right to do so has sent the polling industry into crsisis. On November 15 Bhaskar Chakravorti, Senior Associate Dean of International Business and Finance at Tufts University's Fletcher School blogged: "Predicting the Trump Presidency: How I blew It."[7] In his post Chakravorti wrote:

> *"What happens when the data misleads? Much of the data that various parties drew upon were from the pre-election polls that are now taking a lot of heat. The 'science' of predictive data must be combined with nuance. We have to interpret the data in context. Voters or consumers are not just demographic segments; their choices are guided by a mix of what they know, who they are, what they want and what they believe, hope and fear. Simply equating demographic segments with choices widely misses the mark."*

The major polls – and polls of polls – were so wrong in their common prediction of a Clinton victory that many other pollsters took to the blogosphere in the days after the election to apologize for

---

[7] Huffingtonpost.com, November 15, 2016

the state of polling in general. There is, in fact, real science behind modern polling, but one can't demand equal certainty of all sciences. One must accept the degree of certainty permitted by the subject. As sciences go, polling is an inexact science and its subject matter, human behavior, is squirrely, fickle and at times deceptive. On November 10, *Huffington Post* staff reporter and polling director, Ariel Edwards-Levy, and senior polling editor, Natalie Jackson, posted:

> *"The American Association for Public Opinion Research has a committee to investigate what went wrong with pre-election polling. There apparently was a hidden Trump vote that polls weren't capturing. And low voter turnout helps explain how Hillary Clinton won the popular vote but lost the Electoral College."*

HuffPollster said:

> *"I didn't think there was any way Republican Donald Trump would win. But my presidential and Senate forecasts for* The Huffington Post *badly differed from what played out on Tuesday night and Wednesday morning.... The model structure wasn't the problem. The problem was that the data going into the model turned out to be wrong in several key places."*

It has been noted that multiple political science forecasts were far closer to the mark than poll-based predictions. HuffPollster conceded:

> *"[S]everal very early forecast models constructed by political scientists pointed toward a Trump win, or at least a very close race.... **We may have excluded polls that mattered from our model**."*

But polling inaccuracies weren't really the problem. One can argue that the widely reported predictions of a decisive Clinton win dampened the enthusiasm of some voters, particularly young voters whose enthusiasm was already moistened by the fact that it was Clinton and not Bernie Sanders facing off against Trump. More voters than just the young were put off by that fact and while they probably preferred the prospect of a Clinton victory to the practically unthinkable implications of a Trump presidency, assured by inaccurate polls that their votes weren't needed, perhaps they stayed home.

That's an attractive postulation for anyone not interested in the truth. It was the Clinton campaign that failed to energize voters, not mistaken polls that meant very little to begin with and nothing in the end. In 2008, every poll in the country boldly predicted that Barack Obama would win a historic victory over John McCain by a wide margin and nationwide voter turnout was 63.7%. Those same polls predicted a Clinton victory eight years later and the turnout was 55.4%. The difference was not that one election was historic and the other not. In 2008, a Black man was on the ballot. In 2016, a woman was. Since the difference clearly was not the uniquely historic candidate's standing in the polls, I will suggest at the risk of giving offense that Barack Obama excited young, marginalized, and historically under-represented voters about casting their vote and Hillary Clinton did not.

The overall voter turnout in 2016 was the lowest for any presidential election in 20 years. That reason alone is sufficient to account for why the polls were so wrong. There are no doubt other reasons that people schooled in polling science will ferret out and analyze in excruciating detail. I'm sure those reasons are valid, but they're superfluous. The polls did not assume that so many likely voters would, in the end, opt out.

Believing the polls led Clinton strategists into serious blunders. Clinton staff in swing states reported that in the final weeks of the campaign they were overly reliant on volunteer canvassers to get out the vote. Not only was Michigan understaffed. Reports came in from Wisconsin where state office staff reportedly pleaded with campaign headquarters for prominent Black surrogates to help bring out the comparatively large African-American population in Milwaukee. As Stein reported:

"'There are only so many times you can get folks excited about Chelsea Clinton,' explained one Wisconsin Democrat. But President Barack Obama and first lady Michelle Obama didn't come. Nor did Hillary Clinton after the July Democratic convention. She would go on to lose the state, hampered by lower turnout in precisely the place that had operatives worried. Clinton got 289,000 votes in Milwaukee County compared to the 328,000 that Obama won in 2012."

He added:

"A senior official from Clinton's campaign [stressed] that one of the reasons they didn't do more was, in part, because of psychological games they were playing with the Trump campaign. They recognized that Michigan, for example, was a vulnerable state and felt that if they could keep Trump away — by acting overly confident about their chances — they would win it by a small margin and with a marginal resource allocation."

It was Clinton's mistake to take the polls seriously. It was Trump's correct hunch not to. By refuting the accuracy of the major polls Trump energized his voters, giving them an establishment target at which to thumb their noses – the rigged polling system – and providing them with demonstrable evidence that their votes were vital to overcome a stacked Clinton deck. The more poll numbers rolled in showing Trump trailing in nationwide and key state polls, the more he thundered against the polls, the media that reported on them, and the favored candidate they showed in the lead. While keeping up his anti-poll rhetoric right to the end, he focused virtually all of his resources in the final run-up to Election Day on the blue wall states he had to crack.

Fox News reporter Joseph Weber wrote:

"Donald Trump is moving into Democratic territory in the final days of his improbable White

House bid, hoping forays into Minnesota and Michigan on Sunday [November 5] and Monday [November 6] will give him enough support from still-undecided voters for a come-from-behind victory against Democratic rival Hillary Clinton."

At a rally in Minnesota on Sunday, November 5, Trump told an audience:

"Hillary doesn't come here. ... Don't vote for her... The reason I'm here is because I know what's going to happen in two days. We are going to win the great state of Minnesota and the White House. ... We are going to be great for Minnesota."

Trump did not win in Minnesota, the only Great Lakes blue state that held for Clinton. The rest of the swing states he saturated with his message at the end flipped to red and carried him to victory, all while the polls continued to deceive. Trump did not waste money in unwinnable states, he did not speak to voters in decidedly blue communities and he did not bother with trying to flip poll numbers. He flipped votes and he did that in the following ways.

Divide and conquer

There are approximately 247 million voting age Americans. Donald Trump received more than 61 million votes. I do not think the evidence supports the idea that a quarter of American adults harbor racial ill will. In fact, I think the overwhelming majority of Americans profess to accept the fundamental truth of racial equality and I think those Americans support the idea of an America in which all races are welcome and treated with equal respect and protection under the law.

Having said that, the role of race in Trump's campaign is undeniable and the outcome of the election is cause for pessimism about the state of race relations in this country. As I discussed in the previous chapter, White identity is subtly different from overt anti-minority sentiment. The difference in the two is what allowed so many White voters to support a candidate who expressed profound insensitivity to minority perspectives. Many White Trump voters

39

would say they support Trump's vision for the country and they have no prejudice against people of other races, ethnicities or religions. It is difficult to reconcile those two seemingly contradictory positions, but the human mind has an uncanny ability to maintain contradictions. People see themselves as they want to be seen and for Trump voters it is clear they were able to rationalize supporting a candidate with a hostile anti-minority message while denying they were anti-minority.

On election night, Van Jones called the result of the vote a "whitelash," saying on CNN:

> *"You tell your kids don't be a bully, you tell your kids don't be a bigot... and then you have this outcome. You have people putting children to bed tonight and they are afraid of breakfast. They're afraid of 'How do I explain this to my children?' This was a whitelash against a changing country. It was whitelash against a Black president in part. And that's the part where the pain comes."*

Trump carried a total of six states won by Obama in 2012. The demographics of those states' populations is worth considering. The U.S. population overall is 77% White (including White Hispanics and all other national origins). The states in question all have White populations higher than that average. The share of White population[8] and margin of Trump victory in those states are:

- Florida – 78% White: Trump 49.1% - Clinton 47.8%
- Iowa – 93.9% White: Trump 51.8% - Clinton 42.2%
- Michigan – 80.2% White: Trump 47.6% - Clinton 47.3%
- Ohio – 85% White: Trump 52.1% - Clinton 43.5%
- Pennsylvania – 85.4% White: Trump 48.8% - Clinton 47.6%
- Wisconsin – 88.9% White: Trump 47.9% - Clinton 46.9%

Trump's play to White identity flipped six Obama swing states and resulted in a decisive Electoral College win. In Iowa the flip was

---

[8] U.S. Census Bureau statistics

dramatic, as it was in Ohio. It was less so in Florida and Pennsylvania. Wisconsin and Michigan flipped from blue to red by razor thin margins. There are 465 counties in the six blue-to-red flip states. Trump converted 77 of those. In Florida he only managed to flip three out of 67 counties, the same number he turned in Pennsylvania, where Clinton flipped two counties from red to blue (see image on the following page).

I'm belaboring a point, but before concluding that Whites in those states are racists, consider the fact that Iowa, for example, has a 93.9% White population and in 2012 the state went to Obama with 52% of the popular vote. In 2008 Obama claimed 54% of the Iowa vote. Those outcomes would not have been possible for a Black candidate in a state full of racists. No candidate could be whiter than either John McCain or Mitt Romney. It was not just being pro-White or anti-non-White that turned Iowa or the other swing states listed above. It was White identity politics and Trump's use of a divisive strategy.

Ari Fleischer, former White House Press Secretary under George W. Bush, was asked how Trump did something that Romney, a fellow billionaire, could not. Fleischer replied, "Romney didn't wear it well. Trump said 'I'm a billionaire and I want more of you to be like me.'" It was that appeal, asking voters to identify with Trump, the maverick, shoot-from-the-hip, populist billionaire, that allowed the campaign to divide Americans, pitting a majority-identifying group against a progressive, diverse group of minority sympathizers. That strategy resulted in conquest of micro-regions of the country where mostly labor-class, mostly White subpopulations felt alienated from a mainstream culture that they perceived to be increasingly diverse and hostile to their core values.

The values at stake included conservative cultural mores, Protestant faith, a belief that the U.S. is and should be essentially a White, English-speaking country, the belief that life begins at conception and the sense that a pluralistic America threatens not only middle-class White heritage but also the country's security and economic prosperity. Trump's repeated invocation of the political and media elite as an enemy of the common people and his willingness to make claims about minority faiths, races and nationalities created an us-versus-them dynamic that militarized his

41

following. The net result of that message was racist, even if his voters were not.

What Trump aroused was a perception of otherness[9] as a threat to majority culture welfare. His message came at a time when Jihadist terrorism shared the news with predominantly Black urban uprisings. Trump's candidacy followed closely on the heels of a Supreme Court decision that made marriage equality the law of the land. He occurred at a time when water cooler talk in workplaces around the country included discussion of transgender access to unisex bathrooms. And then of course there was a serving President who did not look like the White majority and whose international roots and passionate defense of Islam as a religion of peace abraded widely held sentiments to the contrary.

Trump's divide-and-conquer strategy worked to perfection in delivering him the only states where he had a chance, as show in the figure on the following page.

---

[9] For an excellent though ideologically slanted account of human otherness perception see Steven Pinker's *The Blank Slate* (Viking, 2002).

Figure 4: Counties in swing states that flipped from 2012 to 2016 – Blue to Red: 78, Red to Blue: 2

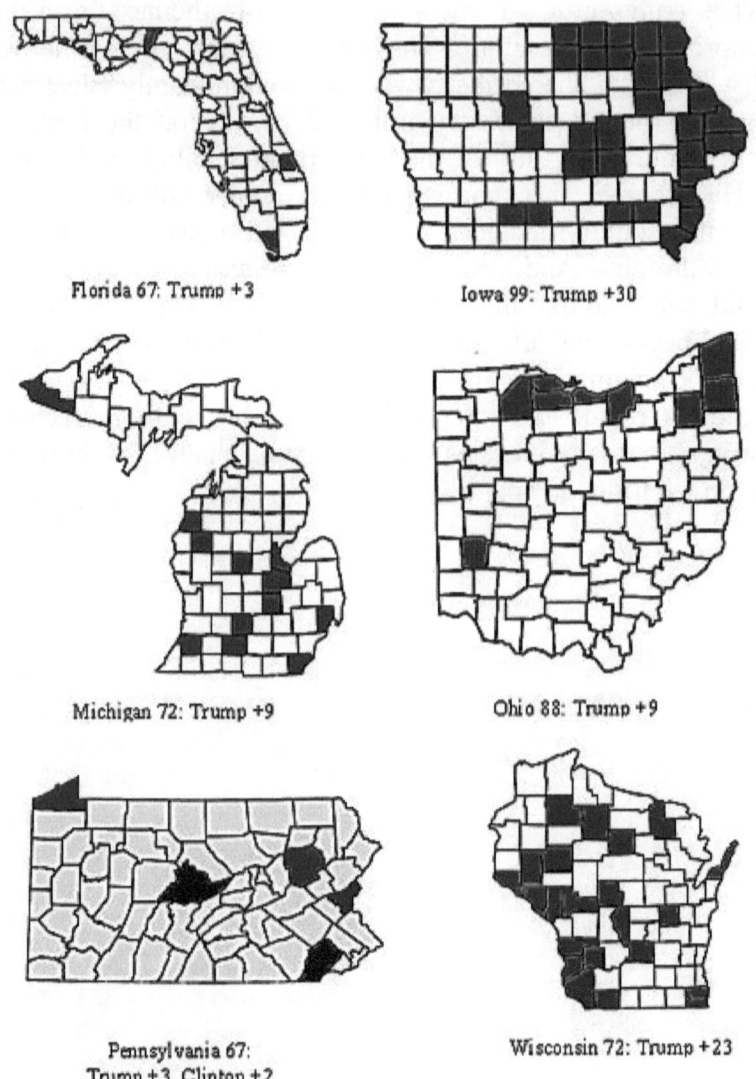

Florida 67: Trump +3

Iowa 99: Trump +30

Michigan 72: Trump +9

Ohio 88: Trump +9

Pennsylvania 67:
Trump +3, Clinton +2

Wisconsin 72: Trump +23

Driving voters to the polls

It's safe to conclude that Trump and his strategists knew from the outset that his electability hinged on his ability to get a highly motivated slight minority of voters to the polls. His only chance at the presidency was to turnout an enormous share of his supporters, converting support in principle to support at the ballot box. We have

43

noted that voter turnout in 2016 was down overall, reaching a 20-year low. Despite that fact, Trump's turnout was nothing short of astounding.

The *New York Times'* Nate Cohn reported on November 9 that:

> *"The traditional view of recent American elections gave even more reason to think Mrs. Clinton was safe. National exit polls suggested that President Obama won the 2012 presidential election despite faring worse among white voters than any Democrat since Walter Mondale. Those polls showed that white voters without a degree were now just one-third of the electorate. It was interpreted to mean that there was not much room for additional Democratic losses, especially once a white Democrat replaced Mr. Obama on the ballot.*
>
> *The truth was that Democrats were far more dependent on white working-class voters than many believed."*

Trump used the strategy and tactics described above to reach a voter base that he then successfully delivered to the polling places in key states in numbers too immense for Clinton's diverse coalition to overcome. As Cohn wrote:

> *"[T]he bastions of industrial-era Democratic strength among white working-class voters fell to Mr. Trump. So did many of the areas where Mr. Obama fared best in 2008 and 2012. In the end, the linchpin of Mr. Obama's winning coalition broke hard to the Republicans."*

Among the bastions that fell to Trump was Pennsylvania's Wyoming River Valley, which Obama carried by more than 10%. Trump won there and secured victories in formerly industrial, White working-class communities throughout the Great Lakes region. Cohn noted:

> *"Youngstown, Ohio, where Mr. Obama won by more than 20 points in 2012, was basically a draw. Mr. Trump swept the string of traditionally Democratic and old industrial towns along Lake Erie. Counties that supported Mr. Obama in 2012 voted for Mr. Trump by 20 points."*

Those flips depended on an energized voting public that was highly motivated to go to the polls by Trump's declaration of war on the supposed forces arrayed against blue-collar America. Voters reacted to the notion that an occult hand of globalism, relativism and post-modern ideals pressed on recent history to the disadvantage of White working-class values, and voters in key areas had reason to believe Trump's clarion call to arms.

In the film *Primary Colors*, a fictitious account of Bill Clinton's first presidential campaign, John Travolta in the character of a Clinton analog tells factory workers in an Upper Midwest state:

> *"I don't have to tell you how hard it is to be looking for work. Hey I don't have to tell you anything about hard times. So you know what I'm going to do? I'm going to do something really outrageous. I'm going to tell you the truth... No politician can reopen this factory, or bring back the shipyard jobs, or make your union strong again... because we're living in a new world now; a world without economic borders... and in that world muscle jobs go where muscle labor is cheap..."*

The real candidate Clinton did not say those words, but they're a close paraphrase of his constant refrain in working-class communities affected by plant closures and off-shoring of manufacturing and other industrial jobs. That message resonated with White voters who Clinton reached with promises to create re-training programs and provide opportunities for displaced workers to obtain 21st Century jobs in a new America. Clinton no doubt meant what he said, but a drive around Flint or Cleveland or Allentown will convince anyone that the promises of the 1990's never materialized for Rust Belt communities. In 1950 Detroit had a population of 1.9

million and was the fifth largest city in the country. Today its population is 677,000 and ranks 21st. Throughout Trump territory in Obama's blue states, one finds disenchantment and a loss of confidence in the public sector.

Democrats did not cause the devastation in former industrial towns and cities. In fact many Democrats fought against the forces that did destroy them – free trade, globalization and deregulation. But to whatever extent Democrats fought on their behalf over the past three presidencies, including 16 years with a Democrat in the White House, working-class White voters in key swing areas did not feel heard by Washington or well-represented by the powers that be. Getting those voters to the polls was not hard for a candidate willing to name their oppressors and attack the establishment with combative invectives.

In Fairfield, Connecticut, Trump told an audience: "I am not running against Crooked Hillary Clinton," Trump said in a speech in Fairfield, Connecticut. "I'm running against the crooked media." In Albany, New York, he said "The system, folks, is rigged. It's a rigged, disgusting, dirty system." The quotes are too abundant to summarize and everything he said made sense to a voting bloc that finds itself unemployed or under-employed, living in a changing country, left behind by history and derided by a coastal elite.

With the Clinton campaign systematically ignoring a significant demographic in critical census tracts, how could Trump not pick off those voters? He picked them off, he invigorated them and he drove them to the polls with enthusiasm to cast their vote for him as much as for anything other than the status quo.

Suppressing opposition turnout

Trump not only brought out his voters; he also kept Clinton's voters at home. Post-election analysis has dwelt on the theme of low voter turnout. Such analysis misses the piece of the picture that matters: It wasn't just low turnout per se that determined the outcome; it was low Clinton turnout.

FiveThirtyEight noted:

> *"The drop in turnout was uneven. On average, turnout was unchanged in states that voted for Trump, while it fell by an average of 2.3 percentage*

points in states that voted for Clinton. Relatedly, turnout was higher in competitive states — most of which Trump won. In the 14 swing states — those where either the winning party in the presidential race switched from 2012 or where the margin was within 5 percentage points — an average of 65.3 percent of eligible voters cast ballots. In the other 36 states and Washington, D.C., turnout averaged just 56.3 percent. That gap exacerbates a tendency for turnout to be higher in the places where candidates concentrate their travel, advertising and other get-out-the-vote efforts."[10]

Forbes' Omri Ben-Shahar was more pointed in his analysis.

"Hillary Clinton was less attractive to the traditional Democratic base of urban, minorities, and more educated voters. This is a profound fact, because Democratic voters were so extraordinarily repelled by Trump that they were supposed to have the extra motivation to turn out. Running against Trump, any Democratic candidate should have ridden a wave of anti-Trump sentiment among these voters. It therefore took a strong distaste for Hillary Clinton among the Democratic base to not only undo this wave, but to lose many additional liberal votes."[11]

Ben-Shahar observed that sure-Democrats who stayed home were responsible more than any other factor for handing the election to Trump. In Ohio, Obama won in 2012 by 350,000 votes and Clinton lost in 2016 by about 10,000. In Detroit and Wayne County alone, more than 75,000 Obama voters did not come out to vote for Clinton.

As far as I know, Ben-Shahar was the first analyst to come across one startling bit of data that makes the issue of low Clinton turnout unarguable.

---

[10] Retrieved from fivethirtyeight.com on November 11, 2016
[11] Retrieved from forbes.com on November 17, 2016

"Wisconsin tells the same numbers story, even more dramatically. Trump got no new votes. He received exactly the same number of votes in America's Dairyland as Romney did in 2012. Both received 1,409,000 votes. But Clinton again could not spark many Obama voters to turn out for her: she tallied 230,000 votes less than Obama did in 2012. This is how a 200,000-vote victory margin for Obama in the Badger State became a 30,000-vote defeat for Clinton."[12]

Certainly Clinton herself bears some responsibility for those voters' passivity. Her strategic and tactical errors and the campaign's basic flaws left some voters uninspired. Polls suggesting an easy Clinton win most likely lulled some of those voters into unfounded confidence. But Trump helped dampen their spirits with a sensational strategy for hyping Clinton's ties to the elite and crushing her would-be supporters' faith in the Democratic Party in general and its candidate in particular.

Trump noted voters' real worries and actual state of affairs blaming both on Clinton and her associations. Time after time he noted that she's been part of the establishment for 30 years and she has done nothing to fix the problems you face. That accusation was patently untrue. In both her public and private life, including 12 years in public office, Clinton has consistently supported progressive legislation and domestic and international charities serving vulnerable people and their interests.

Again, the accusation rang truer than the facts. Working-class In the most economically hard-hit communities in swing states White voters who did support Clinton did so less than zealously. Trump noted her ties to Wall Street, her personal wealth and her comments about ordinary people, most notably her "basket of deplorables" remark. Moreover, he hammered her on the issue of her use of a private email server and other scandals, both real and imagined. He connected her to disgraced characters, including former New York Congressman Anthony Weiner. Clinton and her husband have been

---

[12] Ibid

in the limelight for 40 years and in that time they have had associations with, as Circa.com put it, "felons, thieves, crooked savings & loan owners, an underage sex offender and agents of foreign influence."[13] It's hard to run against your own history of associations.

In June 2016, the *Atlantic* reported on a poll of 2,000 likely voters who were asked to name the two issues that bothered them most about their least favorite candidate.[14] In descending order of frequency, Clinton detractors listed her top five issues as lack of trustworthiness (47%), corruption (39%), propensity to change position on issues (21%), being out of touch with ordinary Americans (12%), and saying one thing but doing another (12%). Other issues that plagued Clinton included not sharing voters' values, being too liberal and various and sundry other traits, all of which were likely amplified in the aggregate mass of Trump voters in key states and probably shared to some extent by would-be Clinton voters who stayed home.

Converting voters

The most universal theme in Trump's winning strategy was flipping voters to his side. No case is more illustrative than Fayette County, Pennsylvania, one of the state's poorest communities where Democrats outnumber Republicans three-to-one. The county as a whole voted for Trump over Clinton by a blistering 30% margin. NPR's David Greene travelled to Uniontown, Fayette's county seat, to talk to voters. Greene reported:

> "*Watching his community decline is one reason lifetime Democrat and retired coal miner Walter Pleban voted for Donald Trump. Pleban hails from a long line of miners and even in retirement still supports the United Mine Workers of America.*
> '*And what we'd like to see, they do something with the coal again because so many people in this area, in our area around here, worked in the mine,' Pleban*

---

[13] Retrieved from circa.com on August 26, 2016
[14] Theatlantic.com, June 17,206

says. 'And now there's a lot of mines closed and there's a lot of fellows without jobs.'"

From another Uniontown voter Greene reported:

"Tina Allen is also a lifelong Democrat who crossed the aisle to vote for Trump. Her husband is a coal miner.

'If he's unemployed, where is he going to go? He's almost 60 years old,' Allen says.

Allen hopes with a President Donald Trump, her husband's mine will be able to stay open and maybe even hire more people. But her main concern is the Affordable Care Act and the high cost of health insurance. Allen says her daughter has high insurance premiums, though she's unsure if that insurance is through the ACA."

Trump was able to persuade even committed Democrats in largely White, largely working-class communities that his plan was more responsive to their real-life issues than Clinton's. If his message was successful in swinging Democrats to his side, how much more effective must it have been with traditional independents? Rightly or wrongly, Trump presented voters with a dramatic distinction between himself and his opponent. To many voters the distinction presented them with an obvious reason to vote for Clinton, contrasted as she was with Trump's odious persona, bigoted rhetoric and shocking ignorance of both the constitutional limits on the presidency and the country's historical and current role in the geopolitical order. For other voters the contrast was as dramatically pro-Trump, casting Clinton as a self-serving member of the illuminati who paid mere lip service to real people's concerns. For a third class of voters the contrast highlighted the undesirable features of each candidate and obscured any virtues either might possess. Those voters stayed home in large numbers and the few who did vote voted for change at any price, even the price of a Trump presidency.

Each Obama voter who voted for Trump counted for a two-vote swing in key states – one fewer for Clinton and one more for Trump.

With that rate of exchange, coupled with low Clinton turnout and a revved up Trump corps, the outcome in tight races was almost inevitable.

Commenting in retrospect, one prominent Republican blamed Democratic Party leadership and the party-wide commitment to a platform that has been eroding steadily for eight years. Former Republican Congressman and House Majority Whip from Texas, Tom Delay, told CNN's Brooke Baldwin, "If the Democrats continue to support their leadership that loses, they will continue to lose." DeLay and disgruntled Democratic staffer Zach, who yelled at Donna Brazile, reached more or less the same conclusion and that's not irony; it's tragedy.

Inherent Candidate Qualities

We have touched on both Clinton's weaknesses and Trump's strengths in the preceding analysis. Clinton's weaknesses were manifest in her tactical miscalculations and her weak overall appeal. Trump's strengths were equally manifest in his use of identity politics, and his ability to rally his voters and keep Clinton's at home. The issue of inherent candidate qualities needs further elaboration. There are some points that are difficult to discuss but ignoring them misses the complete picture of the 2016 election.

President Obama endorsed Clinton in July before a vocal audience in North Carolina. He must have sensed at the time the lukewarm support for the candidate he wished to succeed him. He told the audience of thousands and the world:

> *"You know, Hillary's got her share of critics. That's what happens when you're somebody who's actually in the arena. That's what happens when you fight for what you believe in. That's what happens when you've dedicated yourself to public service over the course of a lifetime. And what sets Hillary apart from so many others is she never stopped caring, she never stopped trying.*
>
> *You know, we're a new country, so we like new things. And I've benefited from that culture, let's face it. When I came on the scene in '08, everybody said, 'Well, he's new.' They don't say that now because I'm*

not. But sometimes we take somebody who's been in the trenches and fought the good fight and been steady for granted."

To Jeff Stein at Vox.com, Obama's endorsement amounted to the argument that Clinton's unpopularity had only to do with her longevity in public life and nothing to do with the "swirl of scandal" surrounding both her and her husband, let alone anything to do with her intrinsic character, personality or political ideas. On July 5, Stein wrote that Obama's opinion was not likely to persuade either Clinton's Republican critics or Bernie Sanders' ardent supporters.[15] As Stein wrote, quoting Obama:

> *"Sometimes we act as if never having done something and not knowing what you're doing is a virtue. We don't do that, by the way, for airline pilots. We don't do that for surgeons. But for some reason, we think for president of the United States, I don't know, who's that guy? Come on.*
> *So, as a consequence, you know, that means that sometimes Hillary doesn't get the credit she deserves. But the fact is, Hillary is steady and Hillary is true."*

To Stein, Obama was arguing that Clinton's weaknesses as a candidate weren't in spite of her strengths; they were the flip side of them.

That does seem to have been Obama's pro-Clinton argument and it was an argument widely accepted by the electorate in general. That argument overlooked some very real issues that were manifest in low voter turnout and the pro-Sanders resistance movement that found its way to the Convention floor in July and never fully dissipated prior to Election Day. The most progressive American voters, especially young progressives, could not put aside their distaste for Clinton.

Clinton had a "tough-on-crime" history that included her use of the now infamous "super predator" line. She has strongly embraced marriage equality in recent years despite a long history of support for

---

[15] Vox.com, "Here's President Obama's 'blunt" explanation for Hillary Clinton's unpopularity," Jul5 5, 2016

traditional marriage that was, according to her own words, "rooted in timeless religious principles."[16] She can be fairly accused of slut-shaming women with whom her husband had well-documented dalliances. Her staff repeatedly referred to Gennifer Flowers as "trailer trash." Juanita Broaddrick has spoken of feeling threatened by then Arkansas First Lady Clinton personally after allegedly being raped by her husband a week prior. She called Monica Lewinsky a "narcissistic loony tune" to reporters. Paula Jones and Kathleen Willey have both spoken to the press about perceived threats and hostility from sources close to the Clintons.

Writing for *The Week*, Michael Brendan Dougherty noted on July 31:

> *"Hillary Clinton has never won a competitive election. This can't be repeated enough. She beat Republican Rep. Rick Lazio for her Senate seat in 2000. And she defeated a mayor from Yonkers in 2006. In her first competitive race, the 2008 Democratic presidential primary, she began as a heavy favorite and she lost.*
>
> *What has she done to improve her chances in that time? She's aged well, I guess. And she served without distinction as secretary of state. The most notable addition to her CV was her strenuous support of military intervention in Libya, which has left that nation in ruins and vulnerable to ISIS. In turn, Libya has left Clinton with a new scandal about her home-brew email server and the deletion of thousands of emails that congressional oversight might have used against her."[17]*

For reasons almost too numerous to list, the 69-year-old Clinton was a bad fit for the increasingly progressive, reform-minded

---

[16] *Washington Post*, March 18, 2013, "How Hillary Clinton evolved on gay marriage," Rachel Weiner

[17] Retrieved from theweek.com, "The astonishing weakness of Hillary Clinton," July 31, 2015

Democratic voters that drove the Sanders campaign to the brink of contention for the nomination. She has always been a centrist, has close ties to Wall Street and has spoken to financial elites for hundreds of thousands of dollars per appearance. Her remark to Anderson Cooper, when asked about her speaking fees, encapsulated her lack of appeals to the new left. At a town hall meeting, Cooper asked if she had to be paid $675,000 for three speeches to Goldman Sachs and in one of the campaign's more tone-deaf moments Clinton answered, "Well I don't know – That's what they offered."

The fact is that Clinton never put away reasonable suspicions that she was a power-trading insider with a history of transactional calculation and use of her position to enlarge her considerable fortune and position.

Dougherty wrote, "Is this really the best the Democrats can do? Yes, and that should worry them."

***

Trump certainly had his own inherent problems as a candidate. He does not speak in linear, intelligible sentences. He displays a child's temperament and attention span. He exaggerates his achievements and denies his many failures. He offends women, racial, ethnic and religious minorities consistently and unapologetically. There is evidence that he is a serial philanderer. He has a spotty business record and a long streak of litigious nastiness. He is a probable tax dodger who still has not publicized his tax returns. He has never held any public office, served in the military or represented any constituency at any level.

The uncommonly eloquent Fareed Zakaria went to the colloquial well for a summation of Trump, the man, calling him "a bullshit artist."

Despite a litany of weaknesses, the one issue that dogged Trump most consistently from the outset was his lack of presidential temperament. He tweeted pithy threats and insults, sometimes at 3:00 in the morning. He spoke off the cuff about matters of which he was clearly ignorant. He cursed and interrupted and hollered and acted in all ways like a frustrated bully lashing out at those who dared to tell the truth about him. All that added up to a marked character deficit in the minds of voter, who preferred Clinton's personality to Trump's by a 58 to 32 margin in a Washington Post-ABC tracking poll on November 6. In the end it didn't matter.

Just as Obama postulated that Clinton's perceived weaknesses were just the flip-side of her strengths, so too Trump sold voters on the notion that the hard edge and flippant self-assurance some found un-presidential were just the obverse side of a man whose strength was manifest in his willingness to jettison politeness for frankness and dispense with political wisdom in favor of common sense. That is the best definition of populism.

Trump is wealthy. That is a strength in the minds of many voters. Trump puts his personal worth north of $10 billion. Reasonable estimates put it nearer $3 billion. Either way he's a wealthy man, a wealthy man with his name festooned on airplanes, skyscrapers and luxury resorts. The fact of wealth does not translate ipso facto to the ability to govern but Trump portrays himself as a man whose empire was built on shrewd negotiating, crafty deal-making and a knack for surrounding himself with talent. Those traits appealed strongly to voters who believed the government has lacked a central focus on their immediate economic interests and who felt like the common rung of politicians were facile, feckless and generally unremarkable. Judging only on the basis of outward shows of material affluence, contrast Donald Trump with, say, Tim Kaine and imagine why disenchanted blue-collar voters in Rust Belt states might gravitate to the former.

Trump has other, less tangible strengths. He's tall. He is a seasoned veteran of reality television, which is, essentially, modern politics. He is brash. His is a thunderous oratory perhaps short on content but long on emotive tone. Trump commands more or less limitless resources and is married to a striking woman with a dramatic aura of her own. His oldest daughter is a legitimate force in the business world and an extremely well-spoken advocate for her father and multiple popular causes.

Those strengths mattered and Trump was keenly aware of them even if some people close to him were not. Early on Trump was criticized for speaking almost exclusively extemporaneously, eschewing scripts and tele-prompters throughout the entire primary season. Time and time again panels discussed when and if Trump would "pivot" to a more familiar campaign style – staying on message, hitting the campaign's key policy points, using rehearsed lines consistently. A few insiders argued from the outset that Trump was best when he was being Trump, but for seasoned observers who could not understand what they were watching, the general assumption seemed to be that, for a general campaign, he would have to switch to a more "presidential" tone and would turn to speaking more from the page and less from the gut.

That expectation saw one moment of validation when, on August 15, he delivered what was promoted as a "major foreign policy address." That speech was almost universally panned, even by Trump supporters. It was flat, uninteresting, and, if anything, intensified the perception that he was ignorant of major policy issues. He read it from the tele-prompter and added almost no typically Trumpish phrasings. His gestures seemed inauthentic and his forced, low-energy delivery was in every way bad television.

The speech itself was quite likely the craft of then Trump campaign manager Paul Manafort, who had promised a post-Convention pivot to networks for weeks. Manafort resigned (i.e. was fired) on August 19th. At the time, Eric Trump indicated that his father simply wanted to go in a different direction than Manafort's strategy was taking the campaign. Plenty of speculation centered on the easy inference that Trump wanted to distance himself from the growing scandal around Manafort, who had allegedly helped to lay the groundwork for Russia's invasion of Crimea and was accused of illegally passing funds to pro-Putin lobbying efforts. That might have been part of the story, but the much bigger part was that Trump could no longer work with any campaign manager not smart enough to let Trump be Trump.

Manafort's successor, Kellyanne Conway, could be seen at times to chafe at some of Trump's most odious public statements and least presidential outbursts both on camera and in social media. But she did have the good sense to stick to her own message that Trump was at his best when he was unscripted. Adding Steve Bannon to the team gave Trump an ally in outrageousness and the post-Manafort campaign, though haunted by the *Access Hollywood* tape and a dozen accusations of sexual misconduct, was an absolute juggernaut. Trump being Trump worked. In fact, of all the strengths one could list for Trump as a candidate, the best by far was his comfort with being what he had always been – a sensationalizing carnival barker with no filter and limitless ego.

Trump's unflappable self-confidence, his comfort in dispensing with the old political rules, his wealth and image, his mastery of the small screen, all these very real strengths not only offset his weaknesses, they also pulled him into a void created by Clinton's issues, failed strategy, weak tactics and inherent flaws as a candidate.

Tie-Ins and Associations

Closely related to identity politics is the tendency for a candidate to be linked to other figures, events, and themes. Arnold Schwarzenegger is a successful two-term Republican governor of a predominantly Democratic state. That fact notwithstanding, he is unavoidably connected to muscle and fitness. He is the Terminator and Conan. For those interested in such things, he is also forever connected to his Kennedy in-laws. None of those associations contribute to his ability to govern but they are never far from the front of voters' minds. For nearly eight years he was "The Governator."

In the same vein, Clinton is linked, inextricably, to her husband's chronic adultery, her own shady deals, big money and power, the Democratic Party machine, a major security scandal, a disgraced ex-Congressman and online flasher, along with a host of long-familiar political figures, each with their own associations. The only things truly fresh about Clinton the candidate were her short-lived, mostly civil dispute with Sanders and her strong dislike of Trump, a man whose 2005 wedding she attended, sitting next to her husband in a front pew. How authentic was her disgust with the man supposed to seem?

Clinton's recent associations include the tragic deaths of a U.S. Ambassador and Information Management Officer at the embassy in Benghazi, Libya, and donations to the Clinton Foundation by various unscrupulous foreign figures in exchange for Clinton's personal attention while serving as Secretary of State. She is connected in the one case to a disastrous lack of preparation and in the other to a perceived pay-for-play policy involving tens of millions of dollars in dirty foreign capital.

Of course it can be contended that Trump shares many of the same associations that tainted Clinton, but Trump owned them whereas Clinton ran from them. In his Convention speech (and on at least a dozen other occasions) he told boisterous audiences, "nobody knows the tax code better than I do and that's why I alone can fix it." He never directly admitted paying no federal income tax for more than a decade, but he didn't deny it and, instead, turned his association with big money and privilege from a negative to a positive. In a debate, he interrupted Clinton's insinuation that he was a tax cheat, saying, "That makes me smart."

Trump is also connected to ostentation and opulence. His home looks like the Hermitage and is perched atop a city that is the beating heart of the world's financial markets. He is associated with beautiful, powerful women, with exotic destinations and a playboy lifestyle. Many of the connections for which he was most heavily criticized were associations a large share of voters approved of. The most obvious example is Breitbart News and its very thinly veiled platform of White nationalism.

There is no credible way to argue that Breitbart is not a podium for alt-right extremism. Under Steve Bannon's direction, Breitbart has become a source of propaganda that promotes White supremacy, Islamophobia, anti-feminism, homophobia, antisemitism, ethno-nationalism, right-wing populist extremism, nativism and a neo-reactionary brand of militant conservatism. By associating with Breitbart, Donald Trump, a former Democrat whose wedding was attended by Bill and Hillary Clinton, a man with no actual conservative bona fides after 40 years in the public eye, managed to connect himself to the alt-right ethos. One of the most widespread criticisms of Trump from the GOP establishment in 2015 was that he was not a real conservative, i.e., not conservative enough. By early 2016, he was linked directly to the extreme right by all commentators on all networks and throughout print media. He co-opted an image. He invented a connection that most politicians run from.

Having taken on the alt-right mantle, he continued to connect himself to figures that would send any career politician in search of cover. When Fox News and Fox Television Stations Group fired its founder, Chairman and CEO, Roger Ailes over a sexual harassment suit that swelled to include allegations from a half-dozen women, Trump tapped him as an advisor. Neither the ignominy of the man himself nor his complete absence of campaign experience mattered to Trump as much as the opportunity to link himself to a powerful conservative icon with a penchant for abusing his position with subordinate women.

Trump is associated with sexism directly and indirectly, including through his public comments on Howard Stern's radio show. Stern and Trump together built on the latter's image from the 1980s as a playboy, with Trump once commenting on the nubile sexuality of his own daughter.

Each time a Trump connection was raised by the Clinton campaign or by an investigative journalist, Trump followed the same pattern. He first discredited the source, often with scathing ad hominem attacks, and then took credit for that association, denying it was a negative at all, the same formula as he employed on the debate stage – "That makes me smart." If figures like Bannon or Ailes are repellent to a significant share of Americans, they're influential with another significant share. Thus while Clinton became a practical synonym for dishonesty and the candidate failed to shake her association with murky scandals and distasteful public figures and events, Trump stamped his own as a synonym for power, associating himself with radical demagogues with nothing to lose who helped to expand and mobilize his base.

Reading the Zeitgeist

To this point in the current century, the authoritative text on White American ethno-politics is *The Rise and Fall of Anglo-America: The Decline of Dominant Ethnicity in the United States*, an oft-cited text from the University of London's Eric Kaufmann. Kaufmann sees a similar thread running through his country's Brexit vote in June 2016 and Trump's election five months later. Kaufmann told Doug Saunders of *The Globe and Mail*:

> *"The general consensus in the literature is that you get the strong anti-immigration sentiment when you have a relatively low local share of minorities and immigrants coupled with a high rate of change... That is, if you live in a very white area but you're close to an increasingly diverse area."*

Saunders wrote on November 12:

"[P]roximity is a bigger driver of extremism than is actual experience: It is not economic decline or immigration that cause people to become right-wing radicals, but proximity to those things, from a vantage of white security that feels threatened by the unknown."

Saunders' editorial ran almost 4,400 words and filled three pages of an eight-page section in a Canadian newspaper. The headlines in that section speak loudly to the general perception of Trump's victory in nations around the world. In addition to Saunders' "Whitewashed: The real reason Donald Trump got elected? We have a white extremism problem," there was a shorter article, five other editorials and three letters to the editor all concerned with the implications of Trump's election. The consensus at *The Globe and Mail* does seem to be that "we," i.e. we Americans, do indeed have a White extremism problem and that sentiment is best summed up by Emory University's Carol Anderson who Saunders quotes: "...[I]f you've always been privileged, equality begins to look like oppression."

There is more to identity politics than racism and there is also more to the zeitgeist than attitudes toward race. It is an unassailable truth that Whites delivered the presidency to Trump and denied it Clinton. Ninety percent of all Trump voters were White and more than half of all White voters voted for him. By contrast, fully 90% of all minority voters voted for Clinton.

It is equally true that voters in diverse metropolitan communities voted overwhelmingly for Clinton and voters in suburban and rural communities went for Trump. Voters with education beyond high school strongly supported Clinton and voters with high school educations or less were one of Trump's strongest demographics.

Given all those facts, we could stick with the raw analytics and conclude, as most analysts have, that the force responsible for Trump's victory was the ethnocentrism of White, ignorant voters in the hinterlands. That would be letting facts get in the way of the story. The whole story is much longer and more complex than raw data can capture.

The week after the election, Trump appointed Bannon his Chief Strategist. A memo from Trump headquarters let it be known that

Bannon would be serving along with Chief of Staff Reince Preibus "as equal partners." The man responsible for elevating the alt-right fringe to the position of viable political ideology will report directly to the president. On November 18, Bannon told *The Hollywood Reporter*:

> "I'm not a white nationalist, I'm a nationalist. The globalists gutted the American working class and created a middle class in Asia. The issue now is about Americans looking to not get fucked over. If we deliver, we'll get 60 percent of the white vote, 40 percent of the Black and Hispanic vote and we'll govern for 50 years. That's what the Democrats missed. They were talking to these people with companies with a $9 billion market cap employing nine people. It's not reality. They lost sight of what the world is about."

Not everything Steve Bannon says is wrong just because he says it. I don't believe most Democratic Party leaders are cozy with billionaires and indifferent to the middle class. But it's clear that plenty of Americans do believe it. Those Americans also believe that the world is less safe than in an imagined Golden Age sometime in the recent past. Compared to that mythical era they believe that America is less Christian, less White, less straight, less prosperous, less powerful in the world and less familiar at home. According to a Public Religion Research Institute poll, 72% of Trump voters believed that American life and culture were better in the 1950s.

The allure of a better time and the possibility of its renewal is a theme as old as civilization. Myth has always accompanied renaissance. Insofar as no one younger than their mid-sixties can even remember the 1950s, it can't be that Trump voters were enlivened by the actual recall of a better time. Instead, they were enticed by the idea that all was not always as it is, that at some previous time people like themselves did not find their environment so unfamiliar, so uncertain and so threatening.

So while Bannon's proclamation to *The Hollywood Reporter* was ignorant, it was nonetheless accurate, especially in the sense that Gingrich addressed: given a choice between facts and what people feel, a politician is well-advised to go with feelings. Ethno-nationalism, economic separatism and cultural regression are parts of the present. They are core values of the zeitgeist that have reached critical mass in England and the U.S. and are increasingly converting nativists in Europe and parts of Asia.

The English voters who rejected the European Union were culturally one with the American voters who rejected continued progressivism under the dominion of an elitist woman with a private school education pledging to continue the policies of a Black president with international heritage and a stated respect for Islam. Both the English and the Americans believed they could make their nations great again. It's not just the "great" part of that equation that matters; it's also the "again" part.

At the most fundamental level, in its original slogan, emblazoned on its materials, repeated by its candidate and spokespeople, the Trump campaign asked voters to help create a new America that resembled a fictitious old one. Many an experienced wordsmith, myself included, derided Trump's slogan as both silly and badly crafted. "Make America great again!" We enjoyed many a chuckle.

And yet that single imperative turned out to be the winning order.

The slogan worked because it distilled into one command all the general topics that had so many voters on edge in the present cultural environment. They hearkened to a leader who called for the restoration of the world they have been imagining for quite some time. In that world marriages resemble those on black-and-white sitcoms. In that world religious difference means Baptist and Methodist. In that world White people have nice homes in safe neighborhoods and they wish no ill on the Negroes in the dangerous city, but they don't welcome them in their homes or schools. The effect is racist, sexist, homophobic, and otherwise intolerant, but the cause was pure nostalgic fantasy.

Although that force permeated the zeitgeist and enthralled Trump's most committed and strident champions, it didn't need to be the prevailing majority view after all, not in the context of large numbers. The most recent reliable Gallup polls show that 43% of registered American voters identify as Democrats, 39% as Republicans. Those numbers are subject to interpretation but for all intents and purposes, in any presidential election of the past century or more, the Democratic and Republican candidates could each count on roughly 40% of the vote.[18] Of the remaining 20% of voters, roughly 5% will reliably go to each of the major party candidates, regardless of voter affiliation. With any Republican and any Democrat each practically assured of winning 45% of all votes, the candidates are fighting over 10% of voters.

As we have seen from the previous maps and blue-red splits, they're fighting over less than that. They're fighting over maybe 10% or slightly more of the voters in six or eight states. That has been the course of recent presidential politics. One must concentrate on swing voters in swing states because the cultural divide that separates blue and red America cannot be breached. A Republican will not carry Massachusetts and a Democrat will not win in Kansas any time in the next generation.

All that being the case, Trump did not need to reach a majority of people through his appeal to a reactionary zeitgeist. He did not even need a significant plurality. What he got was just enough. He was going to get 40% by virtue of being the Republican nominee. He would have pulled off another 5% just by being on the ballot. Those 45% of general voters didn't really have to be wooed, though he did his best. He was going to win 22 states and their 180 electoral votes maybe even if he actually did "stand in the middle of Fifth Avenue and shoot someone."

What Trump got by paying close attention to a reactionary zeitgeist was a theme that resonated with people like the Rust Belt middle-class voters who disproportionately share his campaign's pessimism that things are worse today than before. He reached a large enough share of a minority of voters – actually a share of a minority within a minority – to put him over the top.

The zeitgeist doesn't have to reflect anything. Those whose opinions matter in historical moments don't have to be informed. Democracy is fertile ground for chicanery.

---

[18] The only exceptions is the 1992 election, when Independent Ross Perot won almost 19% of the popular vote.

What Happens Now

I began with the concession that Trump was the better of the two major party candidates in the 2016 presidential election. I have attempted to support that rather dismal claim with sufficient evidence to make the claim stick. Despite everything I've written I am truly alarmed that Trump is the president-elect and I have grave concerns about his program for the next four years. I note the continuing protests in some cities and I commend the protesters, not unreservedly, but I'm getting to that. For the most part, I will say that anyone willing to publicly challenge the possible regression of this country's policies and the ugliness of Trump's rhetoric is on the right track.

We can't help but notice the stepped-up, overt hatred and increasingly rancorous, even criminal instances of racial, ethnic and religious exclusion that have accompanied the past election season and come to a full boil since the election. As of November 26, the Southern Poverty Law Center has tracked more than 700 acts of intimidation, harassment, and in some cases physical threats and attacks against Muslims, Blacks, Latinos, immigrants and LGBTQ people since Trump's election. One of the most shocking was a series of identical hand-written letters sent to local mosques throughout California (see image on following page).

Figure 5: Anonymous letter sent to California Mosques

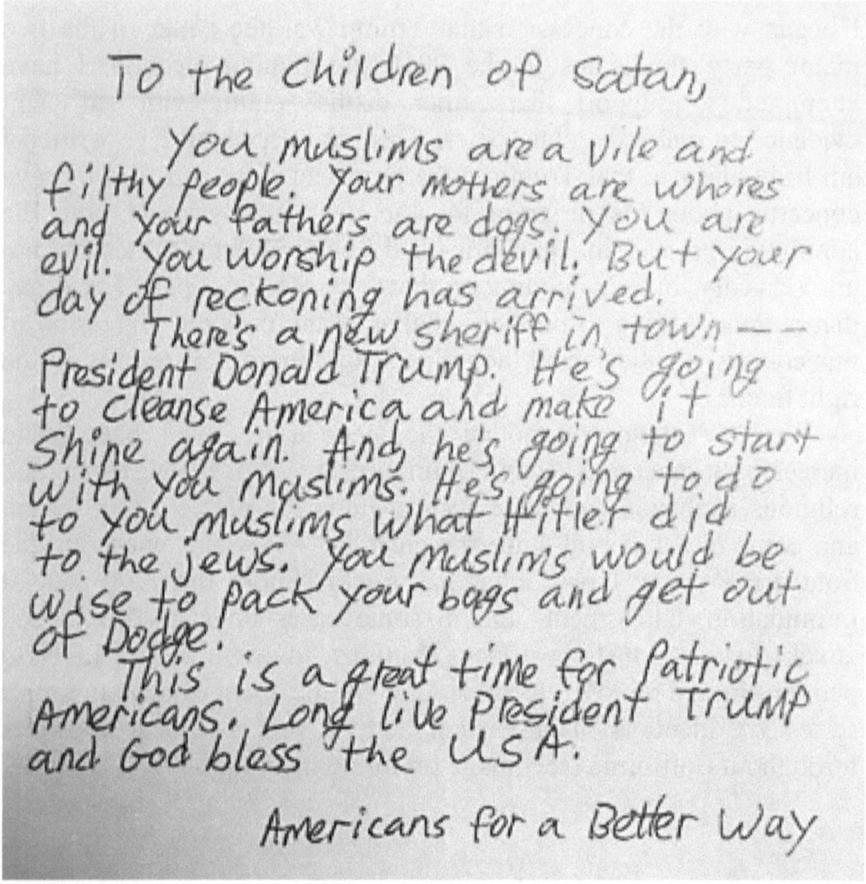

> To the children of Satan,
>
> You muslims are a vile and filthy people. Your mothers are whores and your fathers are dogs. You are evil. You worship the devil. But your day of reckoning has arrived.
>
> There's a new sheriff in town — President Donald Trump. He's going to cleanse America and make it shine again. And, he's going to start with you muslims. He's going to do to you muslims what Hitler did to the jews. You muslims would be wise to pack your bags and get out of Dodge!
>
> This is a great time for patriotic Americans. Long live President Trump and God bless the U.S.A.
>
> Americans for a Better Way

Letters like that are not rhetorical. They are not political hyperbole. They are deliberate, targeted acts of terror and they are increasingly common. They are the byproduct of what can fairly be called the most serious, real and present danger in the advanced world – the normalization of Trump.

The Normalization of Trump
There are and may always be despots, thugs and charlatans in positions of power. There have always been in this country unresolved and unsettling divisions along racial, ethnic and religious lines. There have always been misogynists and preening bully boys who incite others to taunts and jeers at those who cannot defend

themselves. There is nothing at all new about Donald Trump except his acceptability. When a candidate repeatedly threatens to ban 1.6 billion members of a single faith, almost one-fourth of the world's population, from a nation of immigrants, the normal response is outrage, but only until it's no longer normal to be outraged.

We don't have to reach back to the rise of fascism in the 1930s to find warnings of what is at stake. The rise of Vladimir Putin's autocracy in Russia is one clear case. Recep Erdogan's gradually strengthening hold on Turkey and that country's slide into tyranny is another. It is unlikely that Trump is anything like the ruthless, efficient, qualified ruler he purported to be on the campaign trail. It is more likely that he is in completely over his head. Moreover, he probably cannot steer the American government into autocracy in the mode of Russia or Turkey. But there is something else to fear besides the worst possible scenario. Vox's Dara Lind wrote:[19]

> *"Donald Trump probably won't cancel elections, but he could — and is relatively likely to — oversee a sweeping rollback of voting rights. His administration may not throw journalists in jail, but it could easily step up surveillance of domestic protesters. His appointees may not entrench a permanent oligarchy, but it could still — for millions of people in America — reduce the willingness and ability to participate in public life to zero.*
>
> *These wouldn't flout the law; they'd be under color of it and even in concert with it. But they would, nonetheless, be a tragedy for democracy."*

Lind is almost certainly right and that is why it is critical that Trumpism be checked not only if it attempts a blatant assault on American values and Constitutional law consistent with the most extreme fears of the moment. Trump must be resisted in his attempts to affect small changes under the cover of normalcy, small changes with extreme ramifications. But even stalling whatever his agenda might be won't put the horse back in the barn. What Trump has done is quite possibly more egregious than anything he will do. He has

---

[19] Vox.com, November 21, 2016

made a person like himself a valid option for a throng of Americans. He has proven that a crass, unqualified braggart can ascend to this country's highest perch.

In May 2016, Stuart Stevens, Romney's 2012 campaign manager, told Anderson Cooper, "I think one of the greatest dangers of Donald Trump is the idea that he might normalize a speech and an attitude that as a group in America we have decided is unacceptable." It has been six months since Stevens said that and there is no longer any "might" about it. Trump has made the unacceptable demonstrably acceptable to more than 60 million people.

He has also made ignorant, arrogant, vacuous claims legitimate tools in presidential politics. The *Washington Post* published a list of things that Trump claims to know more about than anyone else.[20]

1. Taxes: "I think nobody knows more about taxes than I do, maybe in the history of the world."
2. Tax laws: "I understand the tax laws better than almost anyone, which is why I'm the one who can truly fix them.
3. Social media: "I understand the power of Facebook maybe better than almost anybody."
4. Renewables: "I know more about renewables than any human being on earth."
5. Debt: "Nobody knows more about debt. I'm like the king. I love debt."
6. Banking: "Nobody knows banking better than I do."
7. Money: "I understand money better than anyone."
8. The U.S. system of government: "I think nobody knows the system better than I do."
9. Campaign contributions: "I know more about contributions than anybody."
10. Politicians: "Nobody knows politicians better than Donald Trump."
11. Cory Booker: "I know more about Cory Booker than he knows about himself."
12. Trade: "Nobody knows more about trade than me."
13. Jobs: "Nobody knows jobs like I do."

---

[20] Retrieved online at washingtonpost.com, October 4, 2016

14. Infrastructure: "Nobody in the history of this country has ever known so much about infrastructure as Donald Trump."
15. The military: "There's nobody bigger or better at the military than I am."
16. ISIS: "I know more about ISIS than the generals do."
17. Offense and defense: "I know more about offense and defense than they will ever understand."
18. The 'horror of nuclear': "There is nobody who understands the horror of nuclear more than me."
19. Visas: "I know the H1B. I know the H2B. Nobody knows it better than me."

I hope the *Post* keeps up that list as the Trump presidency brings us four years of spouted expertise.

In his editorial for *The Globe and Mail*, Saunders worried that:

> *"After all, the tragedy this week was not just that a radical faction within the white community broke away from the rest of the United States and elected an extremist, but that they abandoned the Democratic and Republican parties in the process, leaving mainstream politics without a language that can lead to victory.*
>
> *If they want to end this nightmare, they will need to find a way to reach 60 million radicalized white people and find words that can bring them back to earth."*

I disagree with Saunders' assessment only in its numeric estimate. Trump did not sway 60 million radicals, he didn't need that many. Radical White extremists probably number no more than a few million. They might always be with us, as will dangerous lunatics of all colors, nationalities and religions. They are only a small fraction of the problem. It is not the extremism of a few that should concern us: it is the willingness of many to accept conspiracy over fact, to choose emotion over reason, and believe dogma over history. The danger, in short, is not the obvious extremists, those who spout the ugliest vitriol. Those people we can marginalize and avoid. The danger, it turns out, are the tens of millions of generally sensible people who lean toward the extreme because of how it resonates with something they long for, whether or not they will openly shout the hateful rhetoric of dangerous extremists.

The normalization of Trump means the acceptance of irrationality. It means transforming our definition of "presidential." It means ceasing to believe there is anything objectionable about using the most vulnerable people as political pawns and treating the tenets of public propriety as an expendable vanity. At the moment, @realDonaldTrump has almost four million more Twitter followers than @POTUS. That is not a trivial matter. More people are interested in petty little blurts and baseless conspiracy theories than are interested in the official communications of the White House.

The only normal thing about the normalization of Trump is the extent to which normalcy in 2016 encompasses the previously abnormal.

Domestic Policy

Presidents do not make laws. The Legislative branch writes and passes legislation that the president approves or disapproves and even in that regard, the president's power is subordinate to the powers of Congress, which can override a presidential veto. That's what we learn in high school civics, but it's not that simple.

Even though presidents cannot *technically* make laws, they actually do so all the time. One way presidents make laws is by determining what the Congress can enact. It requires a two-thirds vote by both the House and the Senate to override a presidential veto. Two-thirds of both houses is a nearly impossible threshold to reach. Therefore, presidents can pressure legislators to either not pass a given piece of legislation at all or to alter the content of legislation to fit the president's policy priorities.

It is extremely unlikely that the 115th Congress will pass any significant legislation that could be vetoed by Trump. Republicans will have 52 seats in the Senate and approximately 56% of the 435 seats in the House of Representatives. Republican control of Congress actually shrank in the 2016 elections, with Democrats picking up two seats in the Senate and seven in the House.[21]

---

[21] The GOP's narrow margin of control amplifies the significance of Trump's victory. While the party as a whole lost ground, a man with no political

Legislators will, in all likelihood, introduce and pass legislation they have already outlined in the House Republican Program called "A Better Way," championed by Speaker Ryan. The key elements of the program include tax cuts for high earners and corporations, repeal of major components of the Affordable Care Act, reduced funding for Medicaid, deregulation of industry, loosened environmental protection standards, partial privatization of the public sphere and an expanded role for Homeland Security in immigration and law enforcement.

Trump has indicated that he would defer to his vice president for policymaking. Vice President Pence has strong relationships on Capitol Hill, including with Speaker Ryan. It is likely that the major legislative agenda for 2017/18 is already substantially mapped out. Whether or not that is the case, Trump can safely assume that whatever comes to his desk conforms to his policy priorities, at least in the first two years of his presidency

That will mean, almost certainly, bills to gut the Affordable Care Act, to reduce spending on entitlement programs, to open federal lands to petro-chemical exploration and to lower regulatory barriers to predatory lending practices, among many other free-market reforms. It also means there is almost no likelihood of meaningful gun reform, or comprehensive immigration reform, or student loan forgiveness, to name just a few policy casualties.

Signing legislation is not the only way presidents make laws. Presidents also make de facto laws with executive orders. Executive orders have the full force of law with limited exceptions and can direct the internal affairs of government. Executive orders determine how and to what extent legislation is enforced. They also are used to respond directly to emergencies, to wage wars, and to fine-tune policy choices in the implementation of far-reaching legislative statutes.

Some of the country's most historical moments turned on executive orders, reaching back to the first presidency. The only president not to issue executive orders was William Henry Harrison, who died of pneumonia on his 32nd day in office. Franklin Roosevelt issued more than 3,500 executive orders, most of them to respond to

experience defeated the chosen successor of an incumbent president with a 56% approval rating.

the Great Depression. Lyndon Johnson created equal opportunity with an executive order after his predecessor, John F. Kennedy, used an executive order to create affirmative action. Dwight Eisenhower sent troops to Alabama to enforce the integration of Little Rock High School through the power of an executive order. Harry S Truman used an executive order to desegregate the armed forces. The Emancipation Proclamation was an executive order.

Executive orders have been used to wage undeclared wars. Korea, Vietnam and Kosovo, to name a few, were conflicts authorized entirely by presidential executive order. Barack Obama has used executive orders to achieve some truly historic milestones in American policy. The Deferred Action for Childhood Arrivals (DACA) program suspended the practice of deporting "dreamers." Obama used executive orders to raise federal contractor minimum wages and to impose carbon emission standards. His executive order instructing the Justice Department not to enforce the Defense of Marriage Act was a precursor to the Supreme Court's ruling that made marriage equality the law of the land.

Every policy and practice that Obama has advanced under the power of executive orders is threatened under a Trump presidency. Marriage equality is now a fait accompli, but there is nothing to prevent Trump from issuing executive orders to repeal DACA and its counterpart, the Deferred Action for Parents of Americans and Lawful Permanent Residents (DAPA). He has indicated both programs are on his chopping block. He has also said he believes minimum wages are too high. He has not specified exactly which environmental initiatives he will cut, but since the election he has repeated his contention that climate change is a hoax. He also tapped Scott Pruitt to head the Environmental Protection Agency (EPA). As Oklahoma's Attorney General Pruitt sued the EPA on behalf of Oklahoma utilities unwilling to take on the burdens of additional regulation of their coal-fired plants and criticized the agency in a congressional hearing. Pruitt has filed and lost numerous suits against the agency he is now tapped to head. He has also denied that human activity contributes to global climate change.[22]

---

[22] "An Insider's Guide to Oklahoma Attorney General Scott Pruitt's War With the EPA," *StateImpact Oklahoma*, October , 2013.

Trump's executive orders will almost certainly undo much of what Obama did with his. However, as far-reaching as executive order policy-making may be, it is not as long-lasting as the third way that presidents create laws. Presidents make law indirectly through appointments of justices to the Supreme Court. Purists and conservatives will argue that the Court does not, or at any rate *should* not make laws. Whether or not it should, it most certainly does. Supreme Court decisions have determined the law of the land in hundreds of cases. Some of the most notable ended segregation in public schools, guaranteed a defendant's right to legal counsel, legalized abortion and established the fundamental right of same-sex couples to marry. In a sense, eight years of U.S. domestic and foreign policy were also determined by a 5-4 Supreme Court decision that handed the presidency to George W. Bush in 2000.

Donald Trump will appoint at least one Supreme Court Justice to fill the vacancy created by Antonin Scalia's death in February 2016. That appointment will, no doubt, create a 5-4 majority of conservative justices. The implications are far reaching. A newly constituted Court will be poised to hand down rulings on the Affordable Care Act's religious exemptions, collective bargaining rights, immigration rights and affirmative action and much more. Trump has also said he does not consider abortion rights a matter of settled law and could appoint a justice who differs with the legal theory of *Roe v. Wade*.

Foreign policy

Trump's presidency will fundamentally shift the U.S. national identity and affect the country's place in the world. Thomas Wright of the Lowy Institute for International Policy summarized Trump's three core beliefs that will shape his foreign policy:[23] 1. Opposition to America's alliance relationships, 2. Opposition to free trade and 3. Support for authoritarianism, particularly in Russia. To some extent, those three positions are part of the entire Trump package that his supporters most heartily endorsed. The first is a rejection of the old, established international status quo. The second is a commitment to some version of economic isolationism. The third amounts to a

[23] Lowyinstitute.org, *The 2016 Presidential Campaign and the Crisis of US Foreign Policy*, retrieved November 28, 2016

would-be strongman identifying with the strength of a head of state who has put his stamp on the world as an opponent of Western elitism.

American foreign policy is important to the entire world in an unparalleled way. No other nation state can affect the world's military, economic and environmental direction to anywhere near the same extent. At this point, questions outnumber answers regarding how Trump's core beliefs will direct the course of the near future, but the speculation alone is concerning.

In opposing the country's current and historic alliances, Trump upsets a political order that has sustained East-West relations for decades. Trump's aspersion of NATO reveals both a lack of awareness and an absence of appreciation for what that organization has done to prevent global conflict for 67 years. There have been no wars in Europe between major powers since 1945 and was no nuclear exchange between NATO and the now defunct Warsaw Pact. Those are two cornerstone achievements of NATO that determined the course of human history. Peace in the Balkan Countries is the result of NATO collaboration. So is a 75% reduction in piracy off the coast of Africa since 2011. NATO is responsible for intervening in conflicts at the request of the U.N. Security Council that have spared millions of lives and allowed young democracies to take root. Trump could very well undermine the effectiveness of NATO, whether or not he can actually pull the U.S. out of the alliance. Working with isolationist counterparts in a post-Brexit United Kingdom he could render NATO toothless.

Trump has promised swift, massive, decisive action against ISIS. Will he commit ground troops to a conflict in the Middle East? Will he consider the use of nuclear weapons or carpet bombing of ISIS-held territories with large civilian populations? He has said all those possibilities are on the table. He has also said that torture works and has advocated assassinating the families of key figures within ISIS and other insurgent groups.

In a broader context, what will Trump do about engaging terror organizations in general? ISIS and AQAP are the dominant players in the Jihadist movement at the moment, but there are cells and independent terror blocs throughout the Middle East and North Africa, with operatives and sympathizers in major cities throughout Europe, North America and Asia. If it is Trump's policy to "bomb the shit out of them," the U.S. could find itself at odds with most of the rest of the developed world. There is also a very real possibility that Trump could face dissent from his own generals. U.S. military leadership is keenly aware of the delicate balance between military might and statecraft that holds the geopolitical order steady. Presidential orders that contravene international treaties or basic moral principles could be opposed. In fact, since the Nuremburg trials the world has unanimously recognized a codified duty for military leaders to oppose unconscionable orders from heads of state.

A Trump presidency raises serious concerns about global stability and connotes potential conflicts with several countries. Chief among those is China. Trump has all but promised a trade war with China. At stake is a relationship through which the U.S. imported more than $480 billion of Chinese goods and exported $116 billion of its own in 2015. The U.S. currently owes $1.157 *trillion* to China, 30% of all Treasury bills, notes and bonds held by foreign countries. There may be room to improve the trade relationship between the two countries, but a drastic upending of U.S.-China trade would have massive unpredictable consequences.

In early December Trump broke with the U.S. One-China policy by being the first president or president-elect to talk with a Taiwanese president in 40 years. The phone call between Trump and Taiwan's Tsai Ing-wen prompted a swift and condemnatory response from Beijing. In official statements the Chinese government said Trump's conversation with President Tsai reveals the former's ignorance of foreign policy. A front-page story in The *People's Daily*, the official publication of the Communist Party, Beijing warned "creating troubles for the China-U.S. relationship is creating troubles for the U.S. itself."

Anyone old enough to remember the Cold War should be concerned about Trump's position on nuclear proliferation and the use of nuclear weapons. Perhaps it was campaign hyperbole, perhaps not, but Trump has not only suggested that many more nations should have nuclear weapons, he has also suggested he might use them. In August 2016, MSNBC's Joe Scarborough reported that an unnamed foreign policy expert met with Trump months earlier and three times in a one-hour meeting Trump asked, "If we have nuclear weapons, why can't we use them?" But anonymous sources don't testify as clearly as Trump himself to his reckless views on nuclear warfare.

Trump told MSNBC's Chris Matthews he would not take the use of nuclear weapons off the table either in the Middle East or Europe and asked, "Why are we making them if we aren't going to use them?" In March 2016, Trump told Eric Bolling on Fox News that he would not take nuclear weapons off the table in Europe because it is "a big place."

On *Face the Nation* Trump said, "You want to be unpredictable," regarding the use of nuclear weapons, a point he reiterated for Bloomberg two months later. He has said he is fine with the idea of Japan, South Korea and Saudi Arabia having nuclear weapons and told Anderson Cooper, "It's going to happen anyway."

Fortunately there are stop-gaps that stand between Trump's adolescent impulses and the actual launch of nuclear weapons, real human beings, career military leaders sworn to support and defend the Constitution against all enemies, foreign *and* domestic. It is difficult to conceive of a military officer empowered to authorize the launch of a nuclear weapon actually exercising that authority to strike any enemy that does not pose a clear and imminent reciprocal threat to the U.S. or its allies. It is also extremely unlikely that the U.N. will suspend its role in ensuring non-proliferation even at Trump's urging. But even if he cannot or does not act in accordance with his unsettling statements, he has sent a message to the enemies of Western democracy that he might, and that is already a strong motivation for the most radical of those enemies to strike U.S. interests by any means necessary.

The U.S. is also a linchpin in global environmental policy and practices. In March 2016, Chinese Premier Li Kequiang introduced a new five-year plan to achieve environmental goals. Those goals include energy consumption caps per unit of GDP, reduction in emissions of specific chemicals and elements, the addition of volatile organic compounds to emission controls and increased utilization of non-fossil fuels. China is the world's largest emitter of greenhouse gases, accounting for nearly 23% of worldwide emissions, roughly as much as the U.S. and Western Europe combined. China's willingness to commit to intense environmental reform is immersed in a context of global cooperation. A vocal and influential minority of Chinese leadership has continually protested that the West is asking China to forego use of fuels in its industrialization that other countries used in theirs. If the U.S. unilaterally pulls out of international environmental accords, China will likely follow suit.

Furthermore, commitment to the Kyoto Protocol, the Paris Agreement and a multitude of other international agreements is part of America's commitment to international diplomacy and statecraft. The Paris Agreement has 192 parties and signatories. The U.S., China and India account for 42% of all greenhouse gas emissions and 189 other countries have committed to do their share to address an issue that affects all humans regardless of national boundaries. Trump has threatened to withdraw the U.S. from the agreement and his statements have shaken international consensus. At a worldwide conference on November 18 in Marrakesh, Morocco, where diplomats gathered to flesh out details for implementation of the agreement, Mexico's under-secretary for the environment, Rodolfo Lacy Tamayo, told the *New York Times*, "A carbon tariff against the United States is an option for us," adding, "We will apply any kind of policy necessary to defend the quality of life for our people, to protect our environment and to protect our industries."

Global environmental calamity might not follow Trump's inauguration but widespread international discord may.

Climate of Intolerance
The one thing that seems to evoke the greatest concern in the wake of Trump's election is the general climate of intolerance that permeates sections of American society. Trump need not actually build a wall for radicalized voters to feel anger toward immigrants and Latinos. He need not ban Muslims or create an Islamic registry for people to exhibit hostility toward women in hijabs. The ramifications of his polarizing campaign rhetoric are very real, with or without him keeping a single campaign promise.

More than a decade ago, the second President Bush gave a televised speech to the nation on the topic of immigration in which he cautioned Americans against exactly the kind of xenophobia and ethnic intolerance Trump has engaged in, saying:

> *"[T]he vast majority of illegal immigrants are decent people who work hard, support their families, practice their faith, and lead responsible lives. They*

76

are a part of American life but they are beyond the reach and protection of American law...

The United States is not going to militarize the southern border. Mexico is our neighbor, and our friend...

America needs to conduct this debate on immigration in a reasoned and respectful tone. Feelings run deep on this issue and as we work it out, all of us need to keep some things in mind. We cannot build a unified country by inciting people to anger, or playing on anyone's fears, or exploiting the issue of immigration for political gain. We must always remember that real lives will be affected by our debates and decisions, and that every human being has dignity and value no matter what their citizenship papers say."

In 2005, that sentiment still carried weight with American conservatives. The party of Trump appears not to sustain the belief that every human being has dignity and value regardless of their citizenship status. Presidents' words have consequences. After Green Party candidate Jill Stein initiated a recount of votes in Wisconsin, Trump, who lost the nationwide popular vote by more than two million votes, tweeted:

"In addition to winning the Electoral College in a landslide, I won the popular vote if you deduct the millions of people who voted illegally."

and

"Serious voter fraud in Virginia, New Hampshire and California - so why isn't the media reporting on this? Serious bias - big problem!"

The issue is not just whether decorum should preclude a president-elect from blurting out sentence fragments and stamping his feet in a tantrum. The important issue is that the president-elect ought not traffic in patent lies to discredit the American democratic process. Both of the above tweets are not only false; they're decidedly false, pants-on-fire false. But millions, if not tens of millions, of Americans believe them and their false belief adds to the climate of distrust and intolerance that divides the country so completely. Either you believe the president-elect and think the 2016 election was horribly corrupt, or you believe that the president-elect is a recalcitrant liar. Neither of those conditions is desirable for citizens of the most powerful country in the world.

The distrust and division that follow in the wake of Trump's election will find validation. Such is the nature of human belief. As often as not, when reality does not support belief people change reality. What difference does it make that undocumented immigrants are not responsible for wholesale murder, rape and corruption of the political process if millions of people believe they are? Approximately 3.3 million Muslims in America have nothing to do with terror, but that fact is of little consequence if their countrymen believe they do.

American diversity is a source of consternation for sufficient numbers of White, straight, Protestant Americans to create a climate in which non-majority identifiers sense very real hostility. That hostility affects Muslims, Jews, Latinos, immigrants, refugees and asylees, LGBTQ people, women and other historically under-represented groups. White Protestant males, the one subgroup most likely to identify with Trump and his message, make up barely 15% of all Americans. That leaves 85% of Americans, approximately 275 million people, whose identities can be vilified by ethno-nationalist ideas.

The recent history of Black-White relations in this country is enough to warn against increasing division. In 2015, police killed 102 unarmed Black men, nearly two victims per week. In the first 11 months of 2016, 59 police officers were shot to death by suspects while on duty, including three in Baton Rouge and five in Dallas who died in two separate incidents, each perpetrated by a killer reacting to the rash of Black deaths at the hands of police. That sort of catastrophic tit-for-tat could be an anomaly or it could be the tip of the iceberg.

Neutering the Media

Another possible casualty of Trump's presidency could be a free, powerful, objective news media. The independence and objectivity of the American press has been a cornerstone of the nation's stability as a free society. Corruption of the press has likewise been responsible for some of the country's most tragic missteps. As the fourth estate (so dubbed in the 18th Century to distinguish it from clergy, nobility and commoners) the press has been an independent judiciary that has weighed and presented facts, following strict rules of verification and documentation, and presented an unalloyed truth to all citizens, granting them a basis to consent or not consent to the actions of their government.

In the past three generations, the American press crushed McCarthyism, turned American popular opinion against the war in Vietnam, ended the presidency of Richard Nixon, and uncovered a program of domestic surveillance that tracked the communication of hundreds of millions of American citizens. It is hard for most young people to imagine but there was a time in the recent past when the information imported by the major networks was accepted as the unvarnished truth by nearly all Americans. When Walter Cronkite declared the war in Vietnam "unwinnable," President Johnson reportedly said, "If I've lost Cronkite, I've lost Middle America."

Since 1986, the American news media have uncovered the Iran-Contra scandal, released the tape of the Rodney King beating, told the story of Matthew Shepard's murder, revealed the systematic deception behind the Bush administration's run-up to war in Iraq, uncovered the horrors of Abu Ghraib and shared the information leaked by Edward Snowden and Chelsea (nee Bradley) Manning. The course of our history turns on significant news stories that only came to light because of journalistic standards and public trust in the media's fact-based reporting.

Those standards and that trust are deeply eroded. Pew Research Institute reports that 57% of Americans often get their news from television, 38% online, 25% from the radio and only 20% from newspapers. For younger people in particular, traditional media are dying a quick death. Only 5% of people ages 18 to 29 and 10% age 30 to 49 report often getting news from print journalism. Half of each demographic routinely gets news from the internet and for the younger cohort, even television is no longer informative with only 27% of Americans 18 to 29 regularly watching TV news.

The medium of choice is important in predicting the future of reliable, independent, fact-based reportage. By its nature, print journalism provides a platform for longer stories, more in-depth coverage and more intense fact-checking than broadcast media. Television reporting, though offering less in-depth analysis than print, has historically erred on the side of source checking, but its true objectivity is all but gone with the expanding viewership of partisan outlets like Fox News and MSNBC. Even less ideologically slanted networks are drawn inexorably to sensationalism and soundbites. Television is not and cannot be the equivalent of print journalism. Among major American television news options, only PBS stands out as truly committed to hard news and independent analysis. In 2005, 2.5 million Americans regularly watched PBS News Hour. By 2013 that figure was down to 1.3 million, a 48% audience loss in just eight years.

The internet is far and away the most cluttered news space of all. On November 28, 2016, the Daily Kos ran a story that claimed Michigan under-votes were unusually high, feeding speculation that malfeasance was behind Trump's victory in that state, while Breitbart reported in a post from its radio show entitled "Recounts and Vote Fraud" that the vote in Michigan was manipulated to Clinton's advantage. Either one or both of those reports is untrue. The problem is that without in-depth research and cross-comparison, there is no way for a reader to know which report is bogus, or if they both are.

The consequence of such a massive stock of information as is available on the internet is that relevant facts are drowned in the background static of meaningless data. People who get their news from the internet do so in part because it is faster and more readily accessible than print or other media. Doing the research to confirm or refute what one reads online defeats the purpose of opting for convenient news. Thus internet readers are likely to accept the facts that feel right, confirming their own bias with made-up data, and that is as true for those on the left as for those on the right.

In all media, the line between entertainment and information has become so blurred that the term "infotainment" is no longer ironic. For the most part, major metropolitan daily newspapers still clearly distinguish between editorial and reporting and if a story in a reputable newspaper is in the latter category one can be confident it is backed up by fact. But newspapers rely on advertising and advertising follows market share. The very existence of newspapers as we know them is threatened.

At the moment, television is still the dominant news source accounting for Americans of all ages. Television news already shows signs of susceptibility to the allure of Trump's mode of fact-bending. The Daily Beast's Joy-Ann Reid opined on November 26 that the media normalization of Trumpism was already happening.

> *"With Donald Trump about to ascend to the White House, the media risk being tamed by their devotion to access and the belligerencies of the notoriously vengeful resident of Trump Tower and his right-wing wrecking crew of a team. We face a singular test, both as a profession and as a country: will we allow ourselves to see what we see, or will we mentally drape the naked emperor in our midst?"*[24]

The general trajectory of the infotainment-centered media culture is away from investigative reporting and toward feeling-oriented distraction pieces. Trump's methods take full advantage of that trend and his term in office will challenge the public's taste for hard news when diversion is so readily available.

---

[24] Thedailybeast.com, "Already Happening: Media Normalization of Trumpism," November 26, 2016

What to Do Next

I mentioned that I believe young progressives will learn from the outcome of the 2016 election and will not let that outcome be duplicated while they control a dominant share of America's votes. Young voters are not the only aggrieved parties at the moment but they are perhaps the most disillusioned. As Bloomberg's Polly Mosendz noted,[25] there are at least three ways to look at the Millennial vote.

In the first place, voters 18 to 29 voted for Clinton over Trump by a margin of 18%, even though 48% of White Millennials voted for Trump. In other words, young people of color were a major share of Clinton's base.

Secondly, however, 8% of young voters voted for a candidate other than Trump or Clinton, the highest percentage to vote for non-major party candidates since 2000. The youth support for Clinton was lower than for Obama in 2012. Almost exactly the same number of 18 to 29-year-olds voted this year as did four years ago, but fewer voted for the Democratic nominee.

Thirdly, not enough Millennials voted in swing states to win the election for Clinton. Had only Millennials voted, Clinton would have won the electoral vote 473 to 32.

However one looks at it, young voters have especially strong reasons to feel betrayed by the outcome of the 2016 election. The overwhelming majority of young voters who cast a ballot did not vote for Trump and he is now their president-elect. To find a parallel case one has to go back to 1972, the first presidential election following the ratification of the 26th Amendment, which lowered the voting age from 21 to 18. In that election, 52% of youth ages 18 to 21 voted. More than half of them voted for George McGovern, yet Richard Nixon defeated McGovern in the Electoral College 520 to 17. The unrest of 1972 spilled into 1973 and saw the U.S. embroiled in near generational Civil War. The parallels should concern those in the halls of power in 2017.

Millennials might be encouraged to note that by 1973, Nixon was utterly consumed by the Watergate Scandal (thanks to a strong

---

[25] Bloomberg.com, "had only Millennials voted, Clinton would've won in a landslide," November 9, 2016

independent press), his Vice President had resigned under the cloud of corruption charges, his newly appointed FBI director resigned after destroying case files, the Chief White House Counsel was working cooperatively with investigators, and a special prosecutor was appointed to ferret out the facts of the case – all less than a year after the election. Nixon resigned the presidency in August 1974, 20 months into a four-year term.

America does not long abide tyrants.

The Millennial Dilemma

I had the original idea of this book following a conversation with my Millennial daughter and reflecting upon what the next four years will mean for her and her peers. I was convinced to actually sit down and write two nights after the election when a reporter on the streets of Manhattan spoke briefly with a passing protester. The reporter asked the man in his twenties what he was protesting and the protester answered that he was on the streets to demonstrate his outrage that he hadn't gotten a chance to vote for the candidate he and most people he knew so strongly supported. He was referring to Bernie Sanders. The reporter then asked if the protester had voted for Hillary Clinton. He had not. The reporter asked if he thought that might have helped Donald Trump win and the angry Millennial protester answered, "No."

There's no sense quibbling over details. The fact is that one young New Yorker's non-vote had nothing to do with Trump's victory, but we shouldn't let the youngest and angriest generation of voters off the hook. In a general sense, if you did not vote for Clinton you cast half-a-vote for Trump. That is absolutely the case if you are registered to vote in a swing state. I completely understand lacking enthusiasm for the 2016 Democratic nominee. I trust I have spelled out in sufficient detail all the things wrong with the candidate and the campaign. I know I'm in plentiful company stating my opinion that Bernie Sanders would probably have beaten Trump.

But we didn't have that choice. We had the binary choice of a flawed Democratic candidate who Bernie Sanders endorsed, on the one hand, and a singularly unqualified raving egotist, on the other. Jill Stein, Gary Johnson or the write-in candidate of your choice might have been the principled vote to cast, but a vote is not always a statement of principle; sometimes it's a practical, strategic choice.

If you really think a Clinton presidency would be substantively no different than a Trump reign, then casting a vote on principle should be a reward in itself and you have nothing to fear from the Republican president-elect that would not be as terrifying under the Democrat. I doubt that's the case for many young voters. Some Millennials might have had to hold their noses to vote for Clinton, but as opposed to a Trump vote or no vote at all, the scent was a small price to pay.

The challenge for Millennials is to accept the pragmatic in the absence of the ideal. That is a challenge for all generations. Young adults, at all times in all places, are prone to hold out for perfection. Good enough is not good enough for the young. That may be truer now than ever before. More than any American generation before them, Millennials are products of student-centered education. A majority grew up in non-traditional families. They came of age in a period of economic prosperity and grew up sheltered by protective parents. They are the first generation of Americans whose childhoods were scheduled.

All of those things contribute to the Millennial core values. Those values include a sense of civic duty, acceptance of diversity, confidence and willingness to openly question authority. Millennials are techno-savvy and connected to a global community. The breadth of their worldview, often contrasted to their parents', makes them strongly committed to improving the world. The depth of their education makes them keenly aware of what is wrong and encourages them to push for solutions.

But the world might not be perfectible. The Milliennial pushes against an imperfect world demanding perfection and decides nothing else will do. One admires the Millennial impulse but awaits the generation's realization that sometimes good enough has to be good enough. Many have observed this before me. The 44th president said it best. Speaking to a select bipartisan group of college students in 2011, President Obama said:

> "If you're only talking to people who you agree with, then politics is always going to disappoint you. Politics will always disappoint you. You think about some of the issues we've worked on over the last couple of years. I think that the college Republicans

here would say that I was a pretty liberal President. But if you read The Huffington Post, *you'd think I was some right-wing tool of Wall Street. Both things can't be true. What it has to do with is this sense that we have a position and we can't compromise on it. And so one of the challenges of this generation is I think to understand that the nature of our democracy and the nature of our politics is to marry principle to a political process that means you don't get 100% of what you want. You don't get it if you're in the majority. You don't get it if you're in the minority. And you can be honorable in politics understanding that you're not going to get 100% of what you want. And that's been our history."*

It's not just hypothetical. Millennials who stayed home, holding out for perfection, gave Trump a path to the White house. A higher youth turnout in Florida, Michigan, and Pennsylvania alone could easily have handed those states' 65 combined electoral votes to Clinton.

The oldest Millennials will be approaching 40 by the time of the next presidential election. The younger generation already includes parents, homeowners and professionals. Soon the practical concerns of settled life will consume Millennials, pragmatism crowding out idealism. The next time might be the last time this generation of young voters can push American values aggressively at the ballot box by working for the best possible confluence of their deeply held values and viable political reality.

Reclaiming Congress

There will soon be a majority of conservative justices on the Supreme Court not because Republicans will control the White House in 2017, but because they controlled the Senate in 2016. In 2009 and 2010, President Obama worked with a Senate and House of Representatives each controlled by a Democratic majority. In those two years Congress expanded funding for children's health insurance, designated two million acres of federally protected wilderness, broadened the definition of financial crimes, granted the Food and Drug Administration the power to regulate the tobacco industry, created the Consumer Financial Protection Bureau, and passed the Affordable Care Act, among many other achievements. Democrats lost control of the House in 2011 and the Senate in 2013. Since then the president has struggled to sign any meaningful legislation. President Obama's nominee to the Supreme Court has almost 20 years of experience on the Federal Appeals bench and was identified prior to his nomination by leading Republicans as a nominee they could confirm. He will never get a hearing

Midterm elections have consequences. Voters cannot change the occupant of the White House for four more years but they can reconstitute Congress in two. The total voter turnout in the last midterm election, 2014, reached a 72-year low. Only 36.4% of eligible voters voted that year, compared to 58.2% in the presidential election of 2012. In 2014 Democrats lost nine seats in the Senate and 13 in the House.

Low turnout is a problem for progressives. In political science circles the fact that higher turnout helps Democrats win is called the Partisan Effects Hypothesis. Its three propositions are that 1) People who are younger, less well educated, and of a lower socio-economic status are less likely to vote, 2) People who are younger, less well educated, and of a lower socio-economic status are more likely to vote for liberal candidates and thus, 3) Low voter turnout means Democrats suffer as a major chunk of their natural constituency is more likely to be among the non-voters.

Low turnout in the 2018 midterms could be disastrous for progressives. A completely inexperienced President Trump is unlikely to make dramatic headway in his first two years, notwithstanding braggadocio to the contrary. But given a full four years to remake federal policy and sign reactionary legislation, he could accomplish a good deal of his draconian agenda. The Congress is the first and strongest line of defense against a president's over-reach and lawmakers on Capitol Hill have resisted many an authoritarian president in the past.

There are still three Congressional runoffs to be settled on December 10, 2016. Pending the outcome of those elections, Democrats will control either 48% or 49% of the votes in the Senate and approximately 45% of the House no matter what. Those numbers are tantalizingly close to majority control but not close enough. Republicans cannot break a Senate filibuster with their current numbers. However, they can pass spending bills in the House alone, bills that require only 50% plus one vote. Party leaders will most certainly embed language in those bills to redirect, restructure, reduce and even eliminate progressive programs and vestiges of the prior Administration.

If the young progressives in the street today are serious about opposing the Trump administration through the most effective means possible, they will organize to support and elect an opposition majority in 2018. That's a very short time away. In some districts, challengers and incumbents are already looking that far ahead. In the next six months, office seekers will form exploratory committees and begin raising funds. Within a year, they will be hard on the campaign trail. Within 18 months, party primaries will be over and candidates will be chosen for the general election. Thereafter, the television ads, town halls, debates and soundbites will dominate the news and, by then, Millennials in many districts could be stuck choosing between the lesser of two evils.

Or they could get busy now. Democrats need to pick up two seats in the Senate and 24 in the House to reclaim the majority in both. Doing that in 2018 is the best way to check President Trump and bar his path to complete control of the country's policies and programs. Turning over enough congressional seats to regain the majority is a simple solution but not an easy one. Since 1964 incumbent congress members have won at least 85% of their re-election contests in all 27 elections. This year, 97% of incumbent candidates for the House of Representatives won. In 2014 nationwide polls showed that Congress had an 11% approval rating, but 96.4% of incumbents won re-election.

To reclaim control of the House and Senate, Democrats will need to do two things in 2018. First, they must nominate challengers to Republican incumbents who energize and mobilize young voters and other groups with historically low turnout rates in midterm elections. That means speaking to the issues that compelled young voters this year and pushing the progressive agenda that worked for Sanders. Second, they must improve on historical midterm turnout levels. That will require local work to get out the vote – work on college campuses and other community settings as well as strategic local advertising.

For Democratic Party leaders and grass-roots organizers there are choices to be made about where to back such challengers. Fortunately the presidential election map paints a picture that can help make those choices more accurate than just throwing a dart. The two images below show the density of support for Trump and Clinton in states they won. Darker areas represent more support for the winner of each state; lighter areas mean less support.

Figure 6: Density of Trump voters in red states, 2016

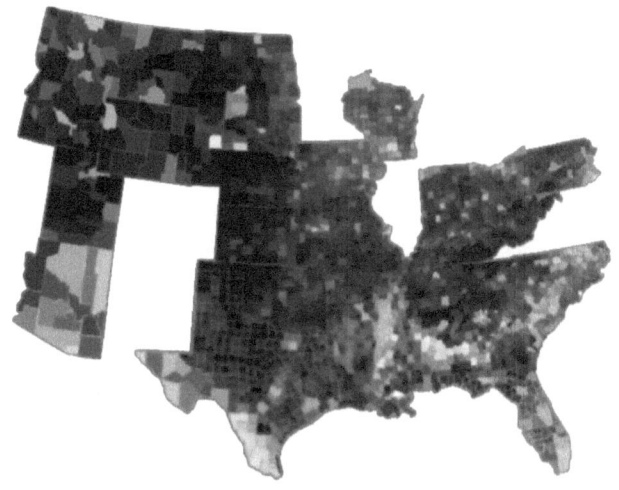

Figure 7: Density of Clinton voters in blue states, 2016

Politics is not chess. There is nothing neat or completely predictable about planning or running a campaign and voters, unlike pawns, knights and bishops, will do as they please. But looking at the maps above one strategy emerges – concentrate your efforts in the lightest areas. That means focusing on areas that were weak for Clinton in blue states and weak for Trump in red states. Chances are, the dark areas are tough places to turn a committed partisan vote. Compare the maps above with the one on the following page, showing the composition of the House of Representatives following the 2016 election.

Figure 8: Map showing 2016 House of Representatives election results for Democrats (black) and Republicans (light grey) including two undecided races in Louisiana (dark grey)

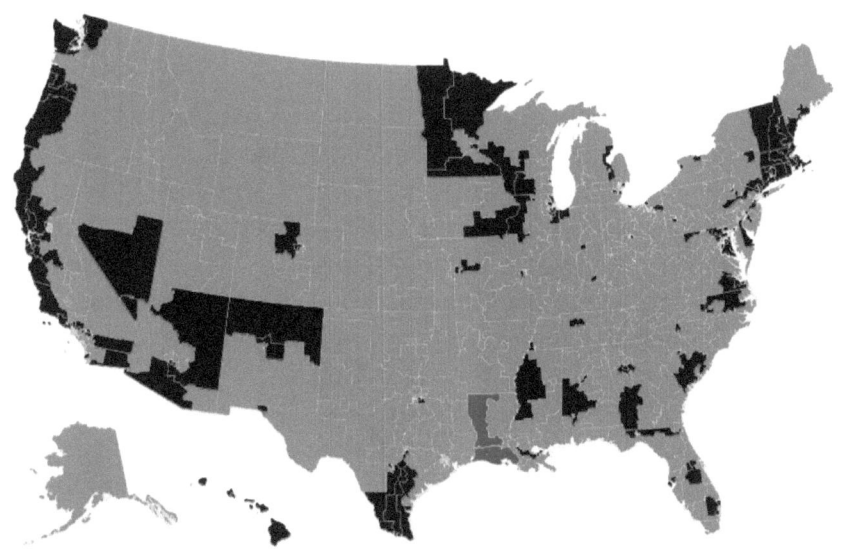

Don't be misled by the vast expanse of light grey. Congressional districts are drawn to include roughly equal populations. Democrats perform much better in densely populated areas and Republicans in rural areas. The map misrepresents Republican dominance insofar as the majority of red territory is more sparsely populated than the blue. But the map does confirm where the Democratic base is concentrated and suggests who that base may be. *The Washington Examiner* reports that the central strength of the party are Blacks and "gentry liberals," a term coined by Chapman University's Joel Kotkin in his book, *The New Class Conflict*. Kotkin identifies gentry liberals as upper-income professionals from the technology sector joined by elites from academia, government, think tanks, and media. What unites gentry liberals, according to Kotkin, are postwar ideals that include environmentalism, consumer rights, and cultural leftism.

As the Examiner points out:[26]

---

[26] Washigntonexaminer.com, "Is this the political map of the future," November 30, 2016

"[B]lacks and gentry liberals by themselves are not a national majority, as the map suggests. And policies designed to appeal to the Obama Democratic base may be repelling other, larger segments of the electorate."

The map tells the story. The third leg of the Democratic base, organized labor, is densely concentrated in the light red and light blue communities throughout the Upper Midwest, where the presidential election was decided. Those communities are, for Democrats, disturbingly red on the congressional map. If Democratic candidates cannot reach working class Whites in those communities, they will likely be a perennial minority in the House and Senate.

Other than the Upper Midwest, Democrats could reasonably hope for gains in Southwest Texas, Florida and North Carolina. Aside from those key regions, successful challengers will come from contests that are ultra-local, targeting vulnerable Republicans, possibly including those tainted by association with Trump.

Politics, as we noted, is far from an exact science and the larger the unit of analysis the less exact it gets. Thinking about the nationwide congressional map is informative on one level and useless on another. It might not be true that all politics is local, but all congressional politics certainly is. Young progressives willing to use the next two years to build a wall against Trump's most heavy-handed ambitions should work to nominate energizing, magnetic, truly progressive candidates for Congress and work hard on those candidates' campaigns against vulnerable Republican incumbents. It sounds simple and it is; but again, it's not easy.

Accepting Compromise

Democratic under-performance among key demographics lost the presidential election, but it also threatens Democrats in general. The problem is that the party is losing its connection to the common voter, the White centrist, socially moderate, fiscally cautious masses in suburban communities, especially communities in former industrial strongholds. Democrats have also seen the defection of a significant share of Latino and Asian voters. There is no chance of flipping the congressional majority by depending entirely on Blacks, LGBTQ voters, and gentry liberals in affluent exurbs. It is not just a matter of Republican sleight of hand; it is a matter of mass defection from what many believe is an increasingly elitist Democratic platform.

Hillary Clinton may be the current poster child for Democratic elitism, but there are other faces of the phenomenon. An issue of *The Nation* summed up the issue in a single headline: "When Liberal Elites Spurn Populism, Trump Happens."[27]

> ☐ *"Even before November 8, it was not difficult to find* [dissent] *among a broad spectrum of the American media, from* Boston Globe *columnist Michael Cohen's dismissal of Bernie Sanders's 'predictable and one-dimensional attack on Wall Street,' to Jamelle Bouie's declaration in* Slate *that Hillary Clinton was right to label Donald Trump's supporters 'a basket of deplorables,' to* New York Times *columnist David Brooks's bland assertion that Trump voters 'are just going with their gene pool.' Way back in September 2015, you could read George Packer in* The New Yorker *sneering at Sanders not only for his 'tendency to drone on like a speaker at the Socialist Scholars Conference circa 1986' but for the sin of offering 'simple answers to difficult problems.'*
>
> *The specter haunting our centrist press wasn't Trump, whose candidacy would never have lasted past the first primary without the constant promotion of a slavish media. Nor was it Sanders, whose insurgent campaign was dismissed and deprecated by the same corporate media that mostly ignored him for as long as possible. No, what really worried the establishment was the people themselves, and the thought that after decades of being offered a forced choice between two paths to their own extinction—the gently managed, technocratically assisted suicide offered by the Democrats, or the savage Darwinian winner-take-all sweepstakes of the Republicans—*

---

[27] *The Nation*, December 5-12, 2016 issue, retrieved online November 30, 2016

working-class Americans might do more than simply
stay home. They might refuse to play along."

It is impossible to quantify something as intangible as "the feeling of elitism," but like all important factors in human choice-making, one knows it when one sees it. Take the case of super delegates – voters in the Democratic primary beholden to no constituency at all. By creating a special voting caste for party insiders and elected officials, the party has practically declared itself to be constructed according to an elitist design. Politicians and party officials wield a power over the party's direction that is denied to the voting masses. That fact played a significant role in Clinton's nomination, as underscored by the disgrace of former party chair Debbie Wasserman Schultz whose behind-the-scenes machinations to boost Clinton's candidacy fouled the process before Democrats could even begin to engage Trump.

On November 29, Sanders spoke to a sold-out house at the Alex Theatre in Glendale, California, and told the audience it would be a mistake to insist that Trump won because his supporters were "racists, sexists and homophobes."

> *"What he touched on in many, many parts of this country is a pain and a level of despair that you never, ever see on television. A lot of people are suffering, a lot of people are hurting and they need a party which brings them into the process."*

Some of the issues at the very center of the gentry liberal platform (among those most hammered upon by Democratic candidates) lack force for many independent voters and Middle American Democrat leaners. Absolute and unconditional defense of a woman's right to make any and all reproductive choices is such an issue. It has become a mantra of the solid left. On the coasts and in the major cities one finds strong support for it. Evidence suggests, however, that it doesn't play as well in the hinterlands. A sizeable share of Latinos rejects abortion absolutism as do many if not most Midwestern White Christians.

Imagine a hypothetical. What if Congress enacted a statute that guaranteed no state could present barriers to abortion on-demand in the first trimester of pregnancy? That might sound like progress toward full, recognized reproductive choice. In fact, such a law could be extremely regressive insofar as it would under-define questions of later term abortions and could be interpreted by a conservative Supreme Court to supervene the *Roe v. Wade* status quo, thus tying the hands of all states, including those with the most permissive laws and policies. *Roe v. Wade* is not settled law, not really, but it is pretty close to the law. How the left goes about codifying it in full terms is a dicey issue, one that could alienate two important parts of the liberal base – religious minorities and Midwestern White working-class Christians. Most social moderates will accept the status quo, but many of them don't want it preached at them.

Gun control is another such option. In San Francisco or Boston, for example, a candidate can go far on a platform of extreme restriction of gun ownership rights. Candidates have been elected in such places having utterly forsworn the Second Amendment. That will not play in Peoria, or in San Antonio, or even Fresno. Outside the major coastal cities, Americans like guns. I suppose Americans like guns everywhere, but in the major coastal cities they'll more easily do without them. Holding out for extreme gun regulation is a losing proposition in rural communities and just about everywhere between California and New England. Even in New England one sometimes has to back down. Bernie Sanders has represented Vermont on Capitol Hill since 1991. It's fair to say there's no one more progressive in Washington. In a primary debate with Clinton and then candidate Martin O'Malley, Sanders spoke of his evolved position on gun control:

> "In 1988, just to set the record straight governor, I ran for the U.S. House. I said, 'I don't think it's a great idea that we sell automatic weapons in this country that are used by the military to kill people very rapidly.' Gun people said, 'Vote for one of the others, but not Bernie Sanders.' I lost that election by 3%. Quite likely for that reason. Do not tell me that I have not shown courage in standing up to the gun people, in voting to ban assault weapons, voting for instant background checks, voting to end the gun

94

show loop hole and now we're in a position to create a consensus in America on gun safety.

It's a country in which people choose to buy guns. More than half of the people in Vermont are gun owners. That's the right of people. I think we have to bring together the majority of the people who do believe in sensible gun safety regulations. Who denies that it is crazy to allow people to own guns who are criminals or mentally unstable? We've got to eliminate the gun show loophole. We have got to see that weapons designed by the military to kill people are not in the hands of civilians."

That is a lesson in compromise. Bernie Sanders, had he the power, would probably rebuild a country without guns in the hands of civilians. But recognizing the strong will of his constituents (*It's a country in which people choose to buy guns*) he accepts what he can get. Sensible limitations on gun ownership are achievable, but not by over-reaching.

The list of "elitist" causes, those of urgent importance to gentry liberals but not to the important voting blocs, includes such things as opposition to fracking and to coal, insistence on self-identified gender bathroom rights, land and wildlife protection, alternative energy research and the like. All those things matter. There's no reason to give up on them but there's no reason necessarily to campaign on them either. Without Democratic control of Congress none of those issues can even be brought to the floor in a meaningful way.

Compromise doesn't mean giving up, but it does mean patience. Young progressives should be focused on getting the right composition on Capitol Hill by whatever means necessary. They might not get everything they want, but progress is achievable in the short run even if perfection is not.

Pushing for Facts

One of the biggest challenges facing all Americans in 2016 is the problem of parsing fact from fiction. The new reality is one in which empty assertions get tweeted as facts, reported as news, debated against other empty assertions vying for airtime and ultimately folded into myth masquerading as information. In his book *Damned Lies and Statistics: Untangling Numbers from the Media, Politicians, and Activists*,[28] Joel Best describes the various means by which unsupported claims enter the public sphere as undisputed fact. One common avenue to putative "facthood" is simple repetition – say something often enough and it becomes so – compounded by media negligence. One example is the case of stalking, about which awareness and concern spread rapidly in the early 1990s.[29] As new media began to take up the topic (fear and salaciousness are great headline grabbers), there were no concrete measures to present the problem in a quantifiable sense. No agencies tracked stalking cases and no studies of the problem had been done. A news magazine reported that researchers suggested some 200,000 people exhibited a stalker's traits.[30]

From there, as Best explains:

> *"[O]ther news reports picked up the 'suggested' figure and confidently reported there were 200,000 people being stalked. Soon, the media began to improve the statistic. The host of a television show declared, 'There are 200,000 stalkers in the United States, and those are only the ones that we have track of.' An article in* Cosmopolitan *warned: 'Some two hundred thousand people in the U.S. pursue the famous. No one knows how many people stalk the rest of us, but the figure is probably higher.' Thus, the*

---

[28] University of California Press, 2012 – The title of Best's book, one of the finest in the field of fact-checking , is taken from a saying popularized by Mark Twain, who attributed the original quote to British Prime Minister Benjamin Disraeli: "There are three kinds of lies: lies, damned lies, and statistics."

[29] Prior to 1990 there were virtually no laws in the U.S. that explicitly banned what is now considered criminal stalking behavior.

[30] Mike Tharp, "In the Mind of a Stalker," *U.S. News & World Report*, February 17, 1992

original guess became a foundation for other, even bigger guesses."

Unfortunately, bad numbers and embellishments on pure speculation don't only appear in daytime talk shows and lifestyle magazines. All too often they crop up in supposedly hard news reporting and, even more often, in politicians' speeches. When Trump contends that millions of people voted illegally he is deliberately nominating a figure for facthood. In that instance his nominee failed. No serious news outlet took the bait and the few sites that did promulgate the claim were panned for their insipidity. But what happens when the news gets it wrong?

News organizations have a responsibility – or once had a responsibility – to disseminate accurate information. Doing so is easier said than done with the trend toward deliberate misinformation that saturates the airwaves and digital platforms. Those news organizations that hew to the old standards for gathering and promulgating only well vetted information too often remain silent when confronted with damned lies and specious statistics.

Prior to each of this year's three presidential debates during the general election season, moderators openly discussed their roles. Prior to moderating the debate in early September, Fox News's Chris Walsh was asked by his colleague, Howard Kurtz, "What do you do if they make assertions you know to be untrue?" Walsh replied: "That's not my job. I do not believe that it's my job to be a truth squad. It's up to the other person to catch them on that."

Walsh can take credit for managing a rancorous, often personal, sometimes vicious exchange. Perhaps it is not the job of a debate moderator to call a lie a lie. But it should be someone's job. Sadly, it's a job frequently left undone.

Politicians like Trump will take credit for the most flattering of false claims, whether or not they have anything to do with those claims or the numbers they purport. On December 1, Trump spoke from a Carrier factory in Indiana where he took credit for saving a thousand union jobs, "and it's going to be more than a thousand, believe me." In fact, it will be 730 union jobs and Trump did not save them. A handout from outgoing Indiana Governor Mike Pence did. The Carrier case is an instructive one for anyone willing to cut through rhetoric and sensationalism in search of facts.

In February 2016, Carrier Corp. and a sister company announced that they planned to close manufacturing plants in Indiana and move their 2,100 jobs to Mexico. The case created a firestorm of social media backlash and was bandied about during election season by multiple candidates as a sign of how American jobs are leaving the country. It's a familiar story, the same one Ross Perot told in 1992, and every presidential candidate since then has pledged to do something about it. According to the U.S. Department of Labor more than 3.3 million American jobs have been lost to outsourcing since 2000.

At this point it is critical to note how numbers can be used to deceive. Yes, American jobs moved overseas *but* there are a net 6.6 million more American jobs today than at the start of the Century. Off-shoring does occur and it no doubt affects a significant share of American households. But it is not the case that the country has lost 3.3 million jobs. One could maintain that we should have added 9.9 million jobs in the past 16 years instead of the 6.6 million we're left with, but that's much too simplistic. Losing some jobs creates room for others and while the U.S. almost certainly would keep more manufacturing jobs, if offshore labor weren't very cheap, the only absolutely certain fact is that more Americans are employed today than ever before.

This is a prime example of sorting fact from fable. The U.S. Bureau of Labor Statistics reports that in November 2016 there were 152 million employed Americans. In 2011 there were fewer than 140 million.

Figure 9: Total employed Americans by month. 2006-2016

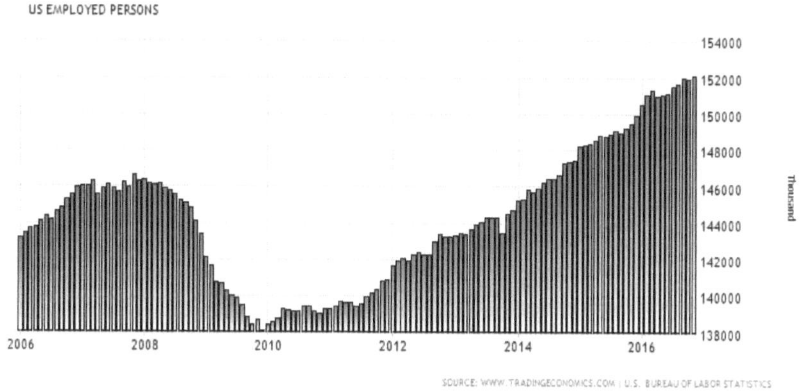

SOURCE: WWW.TRADINGECONOMICS.COM : U.S. BUREAU OF LABOR STATISTICS

98

But in the Post-Truth era, the documented facts of employment matter less than how people feel about employment. As Trump demonstrates routinely, what people feel is that foreigners now do the jobs Americans should be doing and any unemployed manufacturing sector worker can blame his or her plight on a conspiracy hatched by government elites, captains of industry and international dastards intent upon crushing American labor and building up powers hostile to traditional American values. People feel that, but it's false.

At any rate, getting back to the Carrier story: The company announced it would be eliminating 2,100 jobs in Indiana and soon thereafter the state presented options and incentives, including $7 million in tax credits, to entice Carrier to keep those jobs in Indiana. The company at first rejected the state's offer and held its ground until after the election.

Trump famously railed against corporations sending jobs out of the country throughout his campaign saying, "Companies are not going to leave the United States without consequences." No one yet knows what consequences he has in mind, though in the case of Carrier he intimated there might be import tariffs on their goods coming back from Mexico, a condition the president is not empowered to impose.

It came to pass that president-elect Trump, with Pence in tow, appeared at the Carrier plant in the wake of an announcement that he had struck a deal with Carrier to keep half of the 2,100 affected jobs in Indiana. Trump's appearance was the first of many in a 'Thank-You Tour' that kicked off after three weeks of post-election seclusion. The details of the Carrier deal took a few days to come to light.

The deal with the State of Indiana, not Donald Trump, provides the $7 million that were always on the table in exchange for Carrier's agreement to keep 1,150 jobs in the state. Chuck Jones, President of United Steel Workers Local 1999, representative of the affected Carrier workers, points out that the total includes 350 research and development jobs that were never slated to leave the state in the first place. The total also includes 70 non-union supervisory, clerical and office jobs. The remainder includes 70 union positions that will remain in Indiana under the terms of the agreement. Another 1,250 union jobs – 550 from the plant in Indianapolis and 700 from a plant in Huntington owned by Carrier's parent company, United Technologies,[31] will still be sent to the company's plant in Monterey, Mexico. Before Jones corrected Trump's erroneous assertion in a television interview[32], countless commentators, panelists and pundits opined that one had to hand it to Trump – he kept a campaign promise even before the inauguration, which is fine, except for the fact that he did no such thing.

The math is complicated and I won't drag it out, but begin with the fact that the average salary of the affected Carrier workers is $23 per hour, $920 per week. The average wage for all workers in Indiana is $857 per week. In Indiana, unemployment income caps at $390 per week. On average, American workers who lose jobs are out of work for 13.1 weeks before finding new employment. The state income tax rate in Indiana is 3.3% for all incomes. The effective average income tax rate for workers with earnings in the range of the Carrier employees, adjusted down for withholdings and allowances, is approximately 20%.

With all those known numbers it is possible to calculate what the Carrier deal will actually cost. The total cost of unemployment benefits paid to 1,250 displaced workers with an average gap in employment of three-and-a-half months will exceed $6.3 million. The difference in combined state and federal taxes paid by workers making the state average wage versus the union wage they earned at the Carrier plant will be nearly $1 million per year. The $7 million in tax benefits granted to Carrier will be extended over 10 years. Thus, in 10 years the total cost of the Carrier handout will be at least $23.3 million and 1,250 union workers in Indiana will still lose their jobs.

---

[31] Militaryindustrialcomplex.com cites 176 U.S. Department of Defense contracts awarded to United Technologies since 2007 with a total value of more than $23 billion. The list is limited to contracts with a value of $6.5 million or more. (Retrieved December 8, 2016)

[32] In retaliation for Jones correcting him, Trump tweeted on December 7, "Chuck Jones, who is President of United Steelworkers 1999, has done a terrible job representing workers. No wonder companies flee country!" He followed up that attack with another tweet, "If United Steelworkers 1999 was any good, they would have kept those jobs in Indiana. Spend more time working-less time talking. Reduce dues" He has not yet acknowledged the mistaken numbers he used in his speech from the factory floor.

There will probably be fewer cameras at the plant to see workers picking up pink slips than were there to see Trump take credit for a deal that did nothing but privatize gain and socialize loss.

Many will contend, "Yes, but at least 730 families will have a merry Christmas." One could also say, "At least they didn't drown 730 puppies." Both statements are impossible to disagree with and both miss the real point by an equally wide margin. U.S. taxpayers will spend $23.3 million, conservatively, on a deal that hands $7 million in relief to a company that sent 1,250 jobs to Mexico so that a showman could pat himself on the back. Worse still, every CEO in the country now has an incentive to threaten offshoring of jobs unless the government ponies up a bribe. It is Trump's first disastrous deal, but probably not his last.

Finding the numbers I cited above required some time and energy. More than that, it required the interest and willingness to look for them, which in turn required the independence of mind to disbelieve the marketing message from the Trump campaign. That message got repeated unedited by a gullible media in its rush to curry viewers. The deepest truth can be read between the lines in Carrier's press release:

> *"[T]he incentives offered by the state were an important consideration... [T]his agreement in no way diminishes our belief in the benefits of free trade and that the forces of globalization will continue to require solutions for the long-term competitiveness of the U.S. and of American workers moving forward."*

Facts are not common features of partisan sites like Infowars, Breitbart, the DailyKos or countless others. Facts also are in short supply in the rantings of demagogues on both the right and the left. Lawrence O'Donnell is the flip side of Bill O'Reilly. Americans can be excused for being misinformed, given the sheer enormity of misinformation that dominates a polarized infotainment culture, but facts are more readily available today than ever before. Anyone willing to look for them can find the facts that refute the damned lies and statistics that come at us from all sides.

Federal and state government agencies publish real numbers as a matter of policy and in many cases as a matter of law. For the most part, government data is public information and that data is gathered and presented scientifically and without bias. There is no reason to believe Rick Santorum when he says that all 6.6 million net new jobs created since 2000 went to immigrants. That claim and claims like it are subject to easy fact-checking. Santorum also said that the U.S. is approaching "the highest level of immigrants we've ever had." Check either of those claims. They're both absurd. Since 2014, native-born Americans have 4.4 million more jobs and 13.1% of the U.S. population is foreign born, compared to 14.8% in 1890. We are more employed that ever before and have nearly 2% fewer immigrants pro rata than we did in the 19th Century.

Factual claims can be verified or refuted. Regardless of Newt Gingrich's stated preference for feeling and belief over facts, facts do still matter and despite Trump's strong support at the polls, even if 60 million people believe something, it can still be wrong.

Getting Involved

Recognizing an issue does not equal knowing what to do about it. A majority of Americans did not vote for Trump and do not support his agenda. The people already recognize what is wrong, but they did not stop it and now might not know what to do about it. The fact that the problem is far too big for any thinking individual to fix is disconcerting, as is the fact that there is no single issue to be engaged. Progressives share a diffuse blend of core values and agree for the most part about a wide range of issues. But there is, at the moment, no universally accepted platform of American progressivism that enjoys the common, concerted commitment of all adherents – no manifesto of progressive beliefs that sums up the vision and platform of the left.

That, as much as anything else, is how the right routinely beats the left in American politics and why American political power consistently rests with a minority. The right – especially the alt-right – has a clearly articulated worldview that connects its voters. The base that answers the bell for right wing candidates has a big picture in mind that includes cultural and religious values, national identity, economic and foreign policy, and a shared conception of basic relations and institutions. When a self-identified Republican speaks of the party's agenda, he or she is describing a model society distinguished by its difference from the status quo. There is no

102

comparable model that enjoys widespread agreement among typical Democrats or independents.

"Equality, opportunity and fairness," are abstractions often listed by progressive voters as characteristics of their desired America. What those abstractions look like in application is a blurry picture at best. I have spent many a happy hour with progressive friends and colleagues debating not just particulars but also very general questions about just what constitutes equality, opportunity and/or fairness. I don't recall ever reaching consensus.

So part of the problem for young progressives is to do better than their forebears. The New Deal, the Fair Deal and the Great Society are examples of past progressive agendas marked by clear, concrete objectives and outcomes for identified problems. The Democratic Party currently offers nothing like those programs of yore. One hates admitting it, but Baby Boomers and Gen X'ers made the party of FDR, Truman and Johnson into an advocacy society for unfocused gentry liberal causes. The issues that matter to current Democrats and self-described liberals and progressives are all important. Some of those issues are potentially life and death – climate change, water and food security, and much more. Other issues are critical to defining the future of American social life – marriage equality, women's work equity and reproductive choice, LGBTQ rights, ethnic and religious pluralism, and on and on.

But without a clear unity of vision and purpose, listing those issues in a cobbled-together political agenda will not result in the passion and commitment required to defeat a much better organized, though outnumbered, political opposition. That truth and the preceding four paragraphs are well known and expressed by Millennial progressives. The failure of mostly older political leadership to take the truth in-hand and react to it aggressively and definitively is a big reason that so many young voters feel so utterly disconnected from the mainstream and accounts for why so many have looked outside the two major parties for a solution. A vast cross-section of Millennials in all Western democracies doubts their current political leadership and, more importantly, doubts the capacity of any political leadership to make meaningful change even in principle. They deserve to doubt. In their voting lives, Millennial change advocates have seen that the more things change the more they stay the same.

Young voters, take heart – you are not the first generation to feel disenfranchised, disconnected, overlooked and under-represented. Peter Dreier of Occidental College notes that:

> *"[I]n 1900, people who called for women's suffrage, laws protecting the environment and consumers, an end to lynching, the right of workers to form unions, a progressive income tax, a federal minimum wage, old-age insurance, dismantling of Jim Crow laws, the eight-hour workday, and government-subsidized health care and housing were considered impractical idealists, utopian dreamers, or dangerous socialists. Now we take these ideas for granted. The radical ideas of one generation have become the common sense of the next."*[33]

In fact, one doesn't have to look so far back. When the current president was born in 1961, 22 states legally forbade the marriage of his White mother and Black father. In 2003, same-sex marriage was illegal in all 50 states. When change comes, it comes rapidly, but it does not come without hard work. The work will be worth doing if it results in a shift of power and for the time being the most pressing issue is not shifting control of the White House. The issue is shifting local power, including the balance of power in Congress and even more urgently the balance of power in state governments.

There are a total of 99 state legislative bodies in the country.[34] Sixty-eight of those are currently controlled by a Republican majority. Republicans also hold 34 of 50 governorships. In 25 states, Republicans occupy the governor's office and both houses of the legislature, a trifecta matched by Democrats in just six states. Republicans will soon have a 5-4 conservative majority on the Supreme Court. They will control the White House and both houses of Congress, with utter domination of the states. Not to sound

---

[33] Retrieved from MobilingIdeas.wordpress,com, "Social Movements; How People Make History," August 1, 2012.

[34] Forty-nine states have both a senate and a house. Nebraska has a unicameral legislature.

ominous, but it only requires a two-thirds ratification of all 50 states to amend the U.S. Constitution.

To reiterate – the work is worth doing.

Working for change means identifying candidates for local, state and federal offices at all levels. It means campaigning for those candidates, whether for city council, state assembly or the U.S. Congress. It also means not letting internecine divisions among squabbling progressives weaken support for Democratic candidates. As we discussed above, compromise is inevitable. Young progressives need to congeal around a core political platform and accept that candidates may differ at the edges. The important thing is to push for and strongly support the core. Reaching parity with Republicans in control of state houses and congressional representation probably will not mean installing a majority of Bernie Sanders clones in office. But not doing so runs the risk of allowing Republicans to permanently alter the course of American history.

Seek perfection but accept progress. That must be the mantra of the left if it is to upend the current trajectory of American politics. If that means working hard for imperfect candidates then so be it.

Conclusion

Writer and community organizer Saul Alinsky literally wrote the book on political movements. His *Rules for Radicals* (1971) defined and summarized the methods of change and political organizing that shaped the counter-culture movement and continue to inform grassroots activists and seasoned campaign managers to this day.

During the 2016 Republican primary campaign, Ben Carson criticized Clinton for her acknowledgment of Alinsky's contributions, noting the writer's rhetorical invocation of Lucifer as a radical who gained a kingdom. In *Rules for Radicals* Alinsky included an allegorical epigraph that mentioned Lucifer. The fallen angel appeared nowhere in the book's text. As a Wellesley student Clinton did interview Alinsky shortly before his death about his experience in community organizing. Insinuations of Satanism are, one might say, Carsonian.

The interesting fact for our current purposes is not whether Hillary Clinton might have understood and admired Alinsky's rules; it is the extent to which Donald Trump actually used them. For most of the remainder of this book I follow Alinsky's 12 Rules for Radicals as an illustration of how Trump won and Clinton lost. The 12 Rules are not exactly palatable to idealists, but they have been proven time and time again. Any politician or political movement that ignores them will easily fall to them.

***

Rule 1: "Power is not only what you have, but what the enemy thinks you have."
The main sources of power for a traditional political campaign are money and people. Add to that the "earned media" we discussed above and you have the primary units of currency in the political economy. Typically the establishment has ample money but lacks the power of an enthused mass of people. Trump positioned himself as a candidate with limitless money (which he did not ever need to spend) and put the competition on the defensive from the beginning, forcing primary candidates and Clinton to outspend him to get ahead of their perceived deficit. He also packed people into his power base

– not just his staff and volunteers, but also the rally-going public who could identify with him and one another through slogans, chants and goofy red hats. What the enemy thought he had worked to the enemy's disadvantage and freed him to get what he actually needed. In the end he had both.

Rule 2: "Never go outside the expertise of your people."
Complex truths that go over the heads of voters result in confusion and pulling back from the candidate. There is neither time nor patience for lengthy explications of significant positions even in an 18-month campaign season. Most of us on the left lampooned Trump for avoiding discussion of the "real" issues. Trump's genius was in knowing that people don't have deep working knowledge of those issues. He talked about what they do understand and let his opponent talk herself into a hole about things many voters did not understand or care about. Trump only talked about what his supporters knew whether or not those things mattered or were even true.

Rule 3: "Whenever possible, go outside the expertise of the enemy."
How often in the campaign was the Clinton camp caught off-guard by an unscripted or outrageous Trump statement or position? His methods were unforeseen and unconventional but it was the frequency with which he would go off the page that put Clinton's team on its collective heels. Calling for a ban on Muslims entering the country or questioning why Japan does not have its own nuclear weapons were moves for which the Clinton campaign had no counter. It is safe to say that the Trump campaign was completely outside Clinton's expertise while her campaign was well within his.

Rule 4: "Make the enemy live up to its own book of rules."
In 2012, conservative columnist John Hawkins wrote,

> *"This is something conservatives have gotten much better at in the last few years, but we seldom take it far enough. If we did, a tax cheat who advocates higher taxes could certainly never be our Treasury Secretary, Barack Obama would be afraid to associate with race hustlers like Al Sharpton or*

one percenters like Warren Buffet, and Al Gore would
have to either given up his mansion or his status as
the leader of the cult of global warming."[35]

Trump hammered Clinton on hypocrisy, building on a theme begun by Sanders. It's almost impossible to pass as a progressive reformer when you have accepted $675,000 in speaking fees from Goldman Sachs. At every step Clinton was hounded by her own record. She preached transparency and tried to distance herself from her destruction of hard drives and deletion of 30,000 emails. Trump could list a half-dozen foreign influence peddlers whose gifts to the Clinton Foundation gained them an audience with Clinton or her husband. Trump forced her to be judged by the rules of her own book without every committing himself to any rules in the first place. She had almost nothing to hang him on in return and when she tried, calling him a tax dodger, for instance, he could smugly dismiss the charges. The rules didn't apply to him.

Rule 5: "Ridicule is man's most potent weapon."
In naming this rule Alinsky preceded primate behaviorists who have since discovered that even chimpanzees have a sense of embarrassment. He conceded that as a tactic it is crude, rude and mean. But it is also something for which there is no defense. It is irrational and infuriating. Consider the nicknames – "Little Marco," "Lyin' Ted," "Crooked Hillary." Trump was intensely personal and ridiculed his opponents ruthlessly with no filter. It was unprecedented in presidential politics and his opponents flailed for a response.

The fifth rule offends people who believe scruples have a necessary place in politics. It is to Clinton's ethical credit that she heeded Michelle Obama's mandate of going high when her opponent went low. That is the dignified course, but a dignified course to defeat leaves one a dignified loser. If Trumpism is the new normal, the left faces a difficult choice. Will progressive candidates go lower than their opponents? Running clean only works if the unwritten

---

[35] Retrieved from townhall.com, "12 Ways to Use Saul Alinsky's Rules for Radicals Against Liberals," posted April 13, 2012

rules apply to both sides. If they go low and win, going high means standing and dying on principle.

Donald Trump might be the most easily ridiculed man in America. Candidates carved in his likeness will certainly crop up in the very near future. If their opponents are unwilling to fight fire with nastier fire, Republicans willing to resort to ridicule will re-write America's future.

Rule 6: "A good tactic is one your people enjoy."

This sixth rule is entailed by the fifth. A person is usually a moral and decent creature that would not laugh at another's expense. But a person is different from people en masse. A mob is a million-footed bully. The people collectively delight in name calling and no-holds-barred blood sport. A person might not kick a man while he's down, but people will trample him to death. Trump's zealous followers watched to see what he would do and say next. They reveled in his name-calling and posturing. They encouraged and fed off his most extreme improprieties. In short, they enjoyed him.

To be sure many of us enjoyed laughing at him, not with him. But the Clinton team in the main did not invest its energy in making the campaign fun. People did not flock to her and did not hang on her words awaiting the next norm-breaching boast or belittling commentary or shock-loaded declaration. Trump's people enjoyed their candidate in ways Clinton never matched. Trump's people rallied even without urging or coercion. They even invented their own taunts – "Lock her up," "Build that wall."

We naturally avoid things we don't enjoy, like paying attention and going to crowded polling places. But we welcome the chance to involve ourselves in amusement. Clinton did not give independents and conservative leaners any enjoyable incentive to come to her side.

Rule 7: "A tactic that drags on too long becomes a drag."

Alinsky warns, "Don't become old news." Less than a month after the election it is already difficult to remember anything newsworthy that Clinton did or said in her run against Trump. Her media moments were generally reactions to his. Her message stayed unbroken from the time she declared herself a progressive, in an effort to match Sanders' demonstrable progressivism, until the night of her defeat. She was simply old news.

By contrast, Trump said and tweeted new outrages almost daily, claiming the headlines throughout the campaign, never becoming a bore, his every move talked about by supporters and detractors alike. Love him or hate him, he was always fresh.

Rule 8: "Keep the pressure on. Never let up."

Trump never stopped inventing new ways to keep the opposition off balance. He challenged the legitimacy of the entire electoral process. He accused Clinton of criminal conduct and pledged to appoint a special prosecutor to investigate her. He brought her husband's jilted lovers to a nationally televised debate. He never let up.

Clinton, conversely, spent the last few weeks of her campaign doubling down on her own message and largely ignoring her opponent. She let up. She brought out Beyonce and Jay-Z but she let up on Trump. President and Mrs. Obama reiterated Clinton's strengths and hammered old points about Trump but introduced nothing fresh to keep the pressure on him. Following the final debate all the momentum, all the pressure, all the real news made in the campaign was made by Trump who attacked Clinton from new angles. As a result, Clinton's team never had an opportunity to regroup, recover and come out firing. They were used up in fighting back and never pressed the offensive

Rule 9: "The threat is usually more terrifying than the thing itself."

Perception is reality and imagination can foresee consequences far more dire than a candidate can predict. Trump warned that trillions of dollars were at stake and awoke voters' fears that a Clinton presidency would mean the continuation of eight years of policy that left them feeling unheard and overlooked. He trounced Clinton in the fear arena, despite the real terror most leftists have about the prospects for his administration. Fear itself is a powerful motivator. Imagined fear is more powerful still. Like any massive corporate organization would, Trump focused on worst-case scenarios that far exceeded real possibility. That left voters to draw their own conclusions and their conclusions, though they did not comport with reality, led them to vote for the only man who could save them from impending catastrophe.

Rule 10: "If you push a negative hard enough, it will push through and become a positive."

In boxing and politics, the winner is almost always the combatant on offense. Controlling the course of the contest through pushing the action is as important as any other single key to victory. In retrospect, the Clinton campaign was like a boxer content to counter punch and rely on superior training while a reckless, unpolished challenger pressed the fight with a constant barrage of mostly wild punches that set the pace. Judges and voters score in favor of fighters who push their opponents. Clinton spent an inordinate amount of time defending herself against charges she could never put away mostly because Trump never let them go, bringing up scandals, both real and made up, even in response to questions about his own plans. He was constantly on offense, even in the immediate wake of the *Access Hollywood* tape. He defended very briefly, only because he absolutely had to, saying "It was locker room talk." He then turned the entire topic at his opponent with wild, looping punches, noting that no matter what he himself had said or done, it paled in comparison to the wanton depravity of Clinton's own husband. He landed no telling blows but he carried the action. Being on offense at all times let him fight his fight while Clinton fought backing up.

Rule 11: "The price of a successful attack is a constructive alternative."

Alinsky reminds readers of the old saw: If you're not part of the solution, you're part of the problem. This one was hard for Trump. It was a natural enough thing for him to find everything wrong in the country, everything done or not done in the past eight years or the past 30, and blame it all on Clinton and her associates. The challenge, however, was to give voters any concrete alternative. That is Alinsky's challenge – to put something positive in play as an alternative to all the negatives one assigns to one's competition. He struggled through the horrible foreign policy speech and grappled at other times with the expected pivot and what clear policy outlines he would present and he gained his final, fullest stride when he cast aside all the expectations.

The constructive solutions he put in place of Clinton's alleged negatives were sound bite hyperboles, a brilliant strategy for covering his most glaring weakness, his complete absence of an articulate plan. Clinton and her policies were responsible for all unemployed Americans losing their jobs to immigrants so he vowed to build a wall. Building a wall is impractical and prohibitively expensive so he vowed to make Mexico pay for it. Corporations ship American jobs overseas so he promised consequences. That his solutions were vague was not important. They were positive, they were alternatives to the status quo and because they had no detail they were practically uncontestable. He didn't have to defend his alternatives because no credible source could determine precisely what those alternatives were.

Rule 12: "Pick the target, freeze it, personalize it, and polarize it."

For Alinsky, following the 12th rule meant cutting off support networks and isolating the opponent from sympathy. He meant to attack the person, not the institution. People hurt faster than institutions.

Clinton did well enough at identifying her target and freezing it. She made the campaign a referendum on Trump and worked with a mainstream media that turned almost unanimously against him, as did the Republican establishment. He was frozen, almost completely cut off from the support of party elites and traditional political and media standard bearers. But if she polarized him at all, it was to her disadvantage. She argued, in effect, that if you're a Trump supporter you're anti-Black, anti-Latino, anti-gay, anti-Semitic, anti-woman, anti-Muslim and anti-immigrant. That worked on the coasts, where Trump was never in play to begin with. But it failed in the Heartland where people, pushed to a choice between extremes, opted for Trumpism out of ego as much as anything. No one wants to be called a bigot.

In turn, voters driven to Trump's camp by what they perceived to be Clinton's intolerance of their cultural conservatism reacted to his polarizing message that labeled Clinton an insider enemy of the common people. Trump pushed the dichotomy. He argued in essence that Clinton and the liberal establishment have failed to improve conditions for Blacks through policies that encourage dependence. "What have you got to lose?" he asked hypothetical Black audiences. He made much the same argument to all marginalized groups. He did not win with those groups, but he did succeed in polarizing White voters. His message was that liberals believe the country is a racist, unfair society that should coddle and entitle the disenfranchised. Trump reached out to a sizeable share of centrist voters by arguing that Clinton and her ilk do not love America enough to make it great again.

Those are Alinsky's rules. To those I would add one more, one that emerges from our new world.

Rule 13: "Use all available weapons, including new media and alternative platforms."

There is still a prevailing opinion among observers that tweeting is "not presidential." Newt Gingrich has said since the election, "The president of the United States can't randomly tweet without having somebody check it out. It makes you wonder about whatever else he's doing. It undermines much more than a single tweet." Perhaps Gingrich is correct, but if Trump continues to tweet as president, doesn't that make tweeting a presidential thing to do? If Trump proved nothing else in 2016 he proved that the old rules no longer apply. In the new world of politics, taunting and provoking with a tweet, misdirecting the media with a baseless online allegation, revving up the engine of core constituencies with daily one-liners and saturating the alternative media with one's sheer volume of output – all those methods are valid. We might not like them; but they work – and anything that works will most definitely be used until it stops working. Progressive candidates can either get on board or get left behind.

***

The point of analyzing the election through Alinsky's lens is not to belabor the point illustrated earlier, namely, that Trump ran a strategically and tactically superior campaign against a flawed opponent. The point is to note that any candidate could do what Trump did. Probably no candidate will enter politics with more prior media exposure than Trump enjoyed and few will command the personal wealth and resources at his disposal. However, the rules are simple enough. Anyone can follow 13 broad directives.

We should note that the rules were not written for major party political candidates. They were written by a leftist for leftists and they were intended to inform political movements, not campaigns. Yet employing those rules proved as effective in presidential politics as ever before in any venue. Note also that Trump himself frequently insisted that his run to the White House was not a campaign but a movement. He is one of two presidential candidates who made that claim in 2016, the other being Sanders. In 2015 there 18 declared Republican candidates and three declared Democrats. The only two candidates who connected the radical rules of movement politics to a populist campaign were not young upstart radicals; they were White men in their 70s. Something has gone badly awry in conventional party thinking. Young voters are right to be discontent with the powers that be.

The parties either will or will not learn from this year and they either will or will not come to accept that meaningful, important political campaigns *are* movements, they always have been. Change agents are swept into office on waves of populism and their elections are the result of ground-swell activism. That is where the votes come from and how voters get pushed past apathy to dedicated involvement. It will take a movement to react to the movement just concluded. Making Donald Trump a one-term president will require passion, energy and the concerted use of all the rules of social movements. The same applies to reclaiming the balance of power in Congress and the states. Only a movement will suffice.

<u>Stay Tuned</u>
To review, Republicans now hold absolute sway over government at all levels. Any way one looks at the current state of American politics, ours is a country living under total Republican dominion. That's the bad news.

The good news is that parties in power sow the seeds of their own demise. The Republican agenda is extreme and it will inevitably produce extreme consequences, the kind of consequences that cannot be ignored. As a society we can expect, almost certainly, less access to healthcare and higher costs, reduced funding for education, senior programs and services, and no relief from soaring tuitions and crippling student debt. We can confidently predict a destabilized geopolitical order that will spark unavoidable conflict with adversaries both known and unknown. Racial, religious and cultural conflicts within our own national boundaries will escalate. The distribution of American wealth, already its most unequal in the country's history, will we more concentrated at the extremes and the middle class will slip even closer to the poor and further from the rich. Environmental regulation will weaken and corporate polluters will spread and profit. These aren't dire forecasts from a dissenter – they're the logical exigencies of explicit plans already conceived.

In four years Trump will have something he did not have this year, a record. He had no history of public service and had, up until Election Day, done practically nothing in the public arena, certainly nothing to advance the common good. It was a simple thing for him to run against a candidate with a record that included a handful of mistakes when he had neither mistakes nor successes of his own. That will change and there will be documented failures of policy and execution to turn against him.

There is a fundamental difference between conservatives and liberals, including the most progressive of young liberals that typify the Millennial Generation. Conservatives believe strongly in small government and individual responsibility. They believe in free markets and that the role of the government is to preserve individual freedom to make one's own choices. Those are attractive values within reason. However, there is nothing reasonable about the extremes to which the new right pushes those values. It is one thing to believe in personal responsibility; it is something entirely different to believe the community has no duty to assist the individual. It is sensible to want small government; it is reckless to believe the government need make no investment in righting public wrongs or investing in institutions that create opportunities for the disadvantaged.

Liberals, by contrast, believe that government has a positive role to play in creating opportunities and ensuring equal access for all citizens, regardless of their historical disadvantage. They, too, believe in individual liberties, but they believe preserving those liberties does not mean turning over the collective economy to the dog-eat-dog lawlessness of unbridled capitalism. Liberals believe the government must constrain the irresponsible ambition of corporations, enforce regulations, and establish policies to preserve and protect the common good. In all those regards and others, liberals are willing to put the individual second, in some instances, to the group, believing that a rising tide lifts all ships. For American liberals, the Democratic Party has been the long-time bastion of a philosophical tradition that places trust in democracy to correct ills of the past, address issues in the present and plot a course for the future.

I am persuaded that the core beliefs that unite a majority of Millenial Americans will buoy that tradition and mean the end to right wing dominance in American public life. If there is anything that truly unites and defines Millennials, it is their willingness to think outside their own personal interest. Millennials reject the idea that America is an island in a sea of otherness. They reject the belief that corporate entitlement trumps collective interest. They are committed to far-reaching, sweeping reform of basic practices and institutions. They reject the status quo in its entirety and foresee a world where the quality of life is not measured by how much one accretes to oneself, but by how good a world one has to live in. Those values give me hope. They also inspire millions of young Americans.

I will not ask young progressives to work for Democratic candidates just because they're Democrats. Instead, I will urge young progressives to commit their time and energy to re-invigorating the party and reshaping its principles. The only hope of any society is its next generation. Such is the dismal induction of human civilization – a society can't get better until its citizens do so. It is too late to hope that entrenched generations of older American voters will undergo a mass philosophical conversion, but those voters are waning in numbers and influence. The new world with its new technologies, new opportunities, new insights and new values is a world not made for the old. Ours is an Age of Innovation. All that has been is no longer certain and what matters more than anything else is what could be.

The old are sentenced to their own expectations. The possible eludes us. We have only the actual. Of the two, the possible outranks the actual. That is the key awareness that young progressives bring to the American political landscape. How it is now is not how it must be and certainly not how it should be.

Young voters, I'm talking to you. You can deliver us from Trump and open the future to all the possibilities you alone can still imagine. We are all counting on you to live up to your promise. Keep struggling. The future might be on-hold for the moment, but they can't win in the end if you don't let them.